That We Might Have Life

THAT WE MIGHT HAVE LIFE

MARTHA POPSON

NAZARETH BOOKS™
Doubleday & Company, Inc.
Garden City, New York

Nazareth Books is a trademark of Catholic Heritage Press, Inc.

Project Directors for Nazareth Books ™

John J. Kirvan

Roger J. Radley

ISBN: 0-385-17438-1
Library of Congress Catalog Card Number: 80-2080

To
Johnny, Audrey, Andy, Mary,
and Tina

Other titles in series:

With Their Whole Strength
Creed for a Young Catholic
Keeping a Spiritual Journal
A Young Person's Book of Catholic Words
Am I OK—If I Feel the Way I Do?

Contents

Introduction

To be born female and Christian today is to enter into one of the most exciting periods in the history of the world. As never before, women are taking public risks and, in doing so, are changing the face of the earth.

Back in 1870, a United States senator named Charles Sumner told the Congress that "equality of rights is the first of rights." Until all people, male and female, are truly given the same opportunities, that equality will not have been achieved. Each of the women in this book, in her own way, has worked to bring that day closer.

You may have read books about saints who lived in the past. These women and men probably seemed perfect; they never lost their temper or made a mistake. I don't think that was ever really true, but writers used to think that they had to erase all the wrinkles from the lives of the people about whom they wrote. In the process, they also took away much of what makes a saint, or anyone, seem real and human and close.

Each of the women in this book is a flesh-and-blood person who has tried to bring more justice and goodness into the world around her. All but three of them are alive today. From those who preceded us, we can understand that the struggle going on today is not new. For those who are still alive, there are no neat endings to their stories. But life is not likely to be neat. It tends to be messy, so we do not know how the story for each of them will turn out. The important thing for us is to get to know these women and to remember that they tried to make a difference. As you read their stories, notice how the women are alike and how they are different.

I might have chosen others, for there are many more great Christian women than could ever have their stories written in a book.

Take these as a start.

Elizabeth Seton

"Nobody but Riffraff"

1.

Elizabeth Seton and her friends were walking along a dusty road. They had already gone over four miles that morning.

"We will stop for breakfast, soon," Elizabeth promised the others.

Anna Maria, Elizabeth's daughter, called out, "Look at the animals coming to watch us!" Pigs and dogs and geese gave them a noisy welcome as they passed another farmhouse. "They must wonder what kind of creatures we are!"

Elizabeth wondered too, as she laughed along with the others. Here she was, leading a procession of Catholic nuns, along with her own five children, down the road to a new life in Emmitsburg, Maryland.

Certainly little in her childhood had prepared her for this.

Elizabeth was a daughter of one of the most respected families in America. Her father, Richard Bayley, was a famous surgeon in New York, and her mother, Catherine, was the daughter of a well-known Episcopalian minister. Elizabeth was their second child, and she was born on August 28, 1774.

Her mother died when Elizabeth was only three years old, and a baby sister died the next year. Soon her father remarried, and she found herself with seven new brothers and sisters.

Elizabeth and her own sister Mary were sent to Mama Pompelion's boarding school to learn French and music. Elizabeth loved the outdoors, and whenever she got a chance, she hurried outside. She liked to sit and watch the clouds float by. Walking at the seashore, she collected shells, humming a little song as she went along.

From the time she was very young, Elizabeth was interested in religion. She wondered about her mother and sister who had died. She wondered where they were and if she would ever see them again.

She and her school friends were often seen on the streets of New York as they went to visit the sick and the poor. Some of their friends nicknamed them "the Protestant sisters of charity."

Elizabeth wished she could be with her father more often, but his work took him frequently to England. When she was fourteen, he was gone for a year before the family heard from him. News was unreliable, as it depended on the winds to carry the ships back and forth with the mail.

Elizabeth missed her father. She began to feel close to God and prayed to him as "my Father, who will not leave me."

When she was sixteen, her father returned to America. By then, Elizabeth had developed three close relationships with girls who remained her friends for the rest of her life. Julia, Eliza, and Catherine came to visit often.

Elizabeth was pretty and popular. Everyone called

12

her the belle of New York and envied her, but even while she was busy going to dances and parties, she had other things on her mind. She had begun to dream of having a house someday where she could teach children.

Despite her popularity, despite the dances and the parties and the friends, Elizabeth was often extremely lonely. At one time she even thought of taking her own life. She needed to be close to her father, but he was always so busy.

Then something happened in her life. She met a young man named William Seton; they fell in love; and they were married on January 25, 1794, when Elizabeth was not quite twenty years old.

Within the next two years, the young couple became the parents of a daughter, Anna Maria, and a son, named after William. Elizabeth was busy and content with her family. Only her husband's health caused her to worry, for he had consumption, or tuberculosis, which in those days usually meant an early death.

To keep her spirits up, Elizabeth looked forward to visits from her friends. Eliza had traveled to Europe, and she described all the wondrous sights to Elizabeth as they sat together drinking tea.

As she listened, Elizabeth often thought that if she had been a man, the whole world would not have been enough for her.

Then, as she heard Anna and William playing in the garden; as she watched the little ones, Catherine and Richard, coming across the room toward her; and as she thought of the new baby who would soon be born, thoughts of world travel vanished.

13

Elizabeth was well aware of the yellow fever epidemic spreading in New York, and she prayed that her children would be spared. Her father, Dr. Bayley, had worked among the poor immigrants trying to save as many lives as possible, and he had caught the fever himself and died. He and Elizabeth had finally begun to share the closeness she had always wished for, and now that he was gone, she missed him terribly.

Elizabeth was glad when William, who had never been very interested in religion, began to go to church with her more and more. As his health continued to worsen, he turned to the God who was so important to Elizabeth.

In 1803, the couple decided to make a voyage to Italy in hopes that the Italian climate would help William grow strong again. It was also an opportunity for him to see some old friends who lived there. Although Elizabeth was worried about her husband, she was still excited about traveling.

They took Anna Maria with them and left the younger children in the care of the family. The voyage took seven weeks. While they were on the ship, Elizabeth looked forward to walking on solid ground again, to seeing the treasures of Italian art and architecture, and to spending time with their friends, the Filicchis, who would be waiting for them.

Instead, as soon as they docked in Italy, the Setons were put into quarantine for four weeks. The Italian doctors wanted to be sure that they had not brought the dreaded and deadly yellow fever with them.

The trip had been hard on William, and now this

14

extra wait was disastrous. He was weakened by the cold and damp in the cottage where they were forced to stay while they waited. Finally, just in time for Christmas, they were allowed to join the Filicchis.

Barely a week later, William was dead. Elizabeth had watched him suffer in pain for weeks, and she knew that he welcomed the release that came with death. For that, she was grateful.

Even as she mourned the death of her husband, Elizabeth wondered what would happen to her. She was a widow, twenty-nine years old, with five children to raise alone. She didn't know what she could do.

The Filicchis felt sorrow and friendship for this young woman who was so far from home, and it was their example and their kindness that began to lead Elizabeth Seton away from her former life. She had been raised as an Episcopalian, but as she attended the Catholic mass with her new friends, she began to wish she could share their religion. These Italian Catholics seemed so close to God, so comforted by his presence.

When spring came to Italy, Elizabeth was anxious to get home. Somehow, she must make a happy life for herself and her children again. Yet it was not to be as simple as that. The Setons and the Bayleys welcomed her home, sharing her sorrow at William's death, but they did not share her joy when she told them she had decided to become a Catholic.

In the America of the early 1800s, there was much discrimination by members of one religion against another. To her wealthy Episcopalian relatives, Elizabeth's intention to leave the church of her

15

birth was a tragedy. For her to become a Catholic, of all things, was more than tragic; it was a disgrace. Most Catholics in America were poor, uneducated immigrants. How could such a well-bred lady as Elizabeth Seton even think of such a thing?

"Nobody but riffraff are Catholic," sniffed an aunt.

Elizabeth considered her decision for a long time. She had been searching for God's never-changing presence ever since she was a little girl longing for her absent father. She felt that in the Catholic Eucharist she would be joined with her God, never to be separated again. There could be only one choice. On Ash Wednesday, in 1805, she became a Catholic.

In doing so, Elizabeth Seton did more than simply change churches. She also made the difficult choice of cutting herself off from her family and friends.

Elizabeth grew increasingly poor. William had left them no money, and now there would be no help from any of her relatives. Only the Filicchis continued to be kind. They asked her to return to Italy with the children and come to live with them, but Elizabeth wanted to stay in her own country. She had to find a way to support herself and the children.

John Carroll, Catholic bishop of Baltimore, Maryland, had met Elizabeth, and he was aware of the situation of her life as a result of her decision to become a Catholic. When he asked her to come to Baltimore and start a school, Elizabeth remembered the dream she had had when she was eighteen. She gathered her children and, in 1808, headed for Baltimore.

Elizabeth's first school soon opened, and before long, with money from new friends who supported her work, she was able to buy a small farm near Emmitsburg, Maryland. Now there would be room to grow.

By this time, Elizabeth had decided that she would never marry again. She wanted to spend her life serving God by teaching others. Already her school had attracted young women who wanted to dedicate their lives in the same way, and Elizabeth, as their leader, was now called Mother Seton. Besides being mother of her own children, she became the head, or mother, of a new order of religious sisters. They were called the Sisters of Charity of Saint Joseph.

Elizabeth wrote to the Filicchis, "Can you imagine me—the head of an entire order of religious sisters?"

When the Sisters of Charity of Saint Joseph arrived at Emmitsburg and found that their house was unfinished, they pitched in and made the best of it. One of the first things they did was to plant a garden, and every day they milked the three goats. There was little money for food. Coffee, made from carrots, and salt pork were the mainstay of their diet that first year.

The sisters did their own spinning and weaving, but the clothes they wore were old and threadbare. A visiting priest once spotted an especially ragged sister and asked her if she were wearing such run-down clothes as some kind of punishment.

"Oh no, father! These are all I have," she explained.

Even before the house—it was to be called Stone House—was completed, Elizabeth and her sisters were out exploring the surrounding area. They soon found sick people and began to help care for them. As they traveled around, they told everyone they met that a school for their children would be opening within a short time.

The people politely explained that they had no money for schooling. The whites of the Maryland countryside were doubtful enough, but the black people who listened to her couldn't believe that Elizabeth seriously meant to include their children.

"Well, thanks for offering," one mother told her, grateful that this new visitor had at least thought about her children. "Maybe someday, black children will really be able to go to school, too, ma'am."

"Not *someday*," Elizabeth explained patiently to the unbelieving woman. "Your children will be welcomed at our school as soon as it is open."

Soon after the school did open, there were over one hundred students. It was the beginning of a system of Catholic schools that would spread across the United States and set an example for others. Although no one realized it at the time, these schools were to be Elizabeth Seton's greatest contribution. For Catholic immigrants arriving in large numbers during the remainder of the nineteenth century, the Catholic churches and schools were their main haven in a new and often prejudiced land.

Elizabeth's schools were free, and there were free lunches and textbooks.

Perhaps because she was a mother herself and knew little children so well, Elizabeth had a strict rule about discipline. The students were never to be spanked or beaten. If they needed correcting, they were told to sit on a bench beneath a crucifix and think about what they had done. Eventually they would come and tell the teacher that they were sorry. Then, with a kiss and a smile, they would be sent back to class. The children quickly grew to love Mother Seton!

In the beginning, Elizabeth Seton had no idea that things would turn out so well. When she started her school, she was amazed and a little frightened. She realized that if success depended only on her efforts, nothing of value would happen. For her, it was up to God now, who had brought her so far from her wealthy Episcopalian childhood.

She looked at the wooden statue of Saint Joseph that her sons William and Richard had made as a Christmas gift for her.

"We're a little alike," she said to the statue.

The slightly crooked eyes of the saint seemed to grin back at her.

"You're not perfect and neither am I." Elizabeth was laughing out loud now. "But both of us are here in Maryland because of a gift of love."

On September 14, 1975, exactly 156 years after her death, the Catholic Church proclaimed Elizabeth to be a saint. She was the first American-born person to receive this honor.

Sojourner Truth

"And the Lord Called Me Sojourner"

2.

The woman who became known as Sojourner Truth—the woman who fought for the rights of women and blacks—was born a slave. In the beginning of her life, she had no rights, not even the right to have a family name. Her first name was Isabella, and her nickname was Bell, but her last name always depended on who owned her at the time, for slaves used their master's last name for their own.

She was born in Ulster County in upper New York State. The northern part of the United States, as well as the South, had slaves and owners, and by the time Isabella was born, somewhere around the year 1797, slaves had been in New York for almost 150 years.

Isabella's family belonged to a man named Hardenbergh. Her father was called Baumfree, which meant "straight-as-a-tree-fellow," and her mother's name was Elizabeth, although most people called her Mau-Mau Bett. Elizabeth had given birth to twelve children, and she had seen ten of them sold away from her into slavery.

At least she still had Isabella and Peter, the baby. Isabella was always thin and her misty eyes seemed to be looking far away. She and her family lived in

21

the slave quarters in the dirty cellar of their owner's house, and her mother told the children stories during the long, dark evenings. Sometimes Elizabeth told sad tales about the other children who were taken away from her, but she always returned to one main idea.

Night after night, she would tell Isabella and Peter, "There is a God, children, who knows all and sees everything. Even if you are taken away from me, he will be with you."

Elizabeth, called Mau-Mau Bett by her owner, believed in one God who was good and who belonged to both slaves and free people. This belief was one of her few comforts in life. As a slave, she knew that her master could come at any time and take her children to be sold. This happened in most black families, and mothers and fathers were powerless to do anything but watch their children being taken from them.

Isabella's parents couldn't give her much in the way of clothing or food or freedom itself, but they gave her something even more precious. From the very beginning, she had a deep belief in God. Because of this belief, she lived to travel across America to help in the fight for the abolition, or end, of slavery, and to help the cause of women's rights.

When Isabella was nine, her master died. Just as her mother had expected, she and her brother Peter were each sold to different masters. John Nealy, also from New York State, bought Isabella for one hundred dollars.

When Isabella was growing up on the Hardenbergh estate, the language everyone spoke was

Dutch. Now, she was suddenly in an English-speaking household, and because she couldn't understand what was expected of her, Isabella was often beaten for making mistakes. She never forgot how cruel and unfair this was, and even then, she was determined to escape her way of life and to help others live in freedom as well.

All alone, far from her family, she remembered her mother's teaching about God, and she began to pray. She wanted to go home to her mother, but since she knew that was impossible, she began to want a better master, and she talked to God. "If you are so powerful, God, you could do that for me."

Isabella hadn't even considered yet that she could pray that she might not be a slave at all.

Shortly thereafter, she was sold to Martin Scriver. He owned a tavern and the life was busy and gay, without any fear of being beaten. She began to learn to speak English.

About 1810, when Isabella was thirteen years old, she was sold again, this time to John Dumont, of New Paltz, New York. After a few years, she married Tom, one of Dumont's slaves, and they had children together. Isabella had given life to the babies, but they still belonged to Dumont, her master. Legally, they were his property, just as if they were horses or cattle. Isabella hated to see this happen to her own children, but she didn't know what else to do.

Then the blacks of New York State began to hear something that gave them a small glimmer of hope. A law had been passed which said that on July 4, 1827, the slaves of New York State would be freed.

People in the North were beginning to agree that slavery was a great evil.

Dumont had promised Isabella that she could go free a year earlier, as a reward for being such a faithful servant, but when the time came, he changed his mind. Yet Isabella could wait no longer. She ran away.

She asked for help at the home of Isaac and Maria Van Wagener, who did not believe in slavery. When Dumont found Isabella hiding there and tried to take her back, the Van Wageners bought her from him and set her free immediately. It was almost hard to believe that she was no longer a slave!

But what about her youngest child, Peter, who had been left behind on Dumont's property? She wasn't worried because a New York law forbade the sale of slaves across state lines. In a year, when all the slaves in the state were free, she would go to Dumont's farm and take him.

She trusted that Dumont would obey the law, but she was wrong. She learned that Peter, who was five years old, had been sold and sent to Alabama.

Isabella was frantic. Even in New York, blacks had heard how hard life was for the slaves of the South. She must get her son back no matter what!

What Isabella did next was the beginning of a fight for freedom that would take up the rest of her life. She took her son's owner to court. He had broken the law by taking Peter out of New York State. The blacks who heard about this were amazed. The white people were shocked. They wondered just who this uppity black woman was to think she could change the way things had been for years.

For Isabella, the answer was simple. She had asked God's help. She had prayed that he would send her a new master, and she had been sold. Surely the same God could take care of one little boy.

"The Lord is on my side," she would say to anyone who tried to discourage her, and after a long court battle, Peter was returned from Alabama.

The people who heard the news could scarcely believe it. Maybe there *was* hope for black families!

Isabella wanted to get away from the scene of so much sadness, so in 1829 she took Peter and moved to New York City, where she found work as a housekeeper. They lived in the city for ten years. Then Peter became a sailor and went off to sea.

With Peter gone, she began to wonder why she stayed in the noisy city, and one morning in 1843, she put her few belongings in a pillowcase and left.

Her employer asked her, "Where are you going?"

"East," she replied, as if that explained everything. "The Lord told me to go East. I must go. I must be about my Father's business."

Another new chapter in her life was beginning. Isabella thought she had heard God's voice before, and she had always obeyed. This time was no different.

The voice also told her to begin this new life with a new name. She walked along the dusty road wondering what the new name would be, and suddenly, she knew the name she would keep for the rest of her life.

"Sojourner! That's it!" she said happily. A sojourner is someone who wanders from place to place and never stays anywhere for long. She would always keep on the move.

Whenever anyone asked her where she got her name, she would answer, "And the Lord called me Sojourner."

For a new last name, she prayed to God again. She needed just the right one.

All at once she decided "Truth" would be her last name. She was so excited that she jumped for joy. No more slave name for her. No more masters who could change it whenever they wished.

She stopped where she was and prayed. "Thank you, God. That is a good name. You are my last Master and your name is Truth. I will be Sojourner Truth until I die."

Armed with her new name and a belief in a powerful God who answered prayers Sojourner wandered along the East Coast.

She was a natural speaker, and she joined the crowds at many of the meetings that were being held on the slavery question during the years just before the start of the Civil War. She never forgot the horror of her early life, and she fervently wanted to bring an end to the system that had approved of it.

As she traveled, she began to become interested in another problem: women, even if they were white, were not allowed to vote. To Sojourner, just as slavery was a sin, this was a sin against the God who made all people equal. In 1852, she attended a Women's Rights Convention in Akron, Ohio.

Some people didn't think that a black woman who was known in the fight against slavery should be allowed to speak.

"We have enough trouble getting people to listen to white women. It'll turn them against us for sure if they think we're mixed up in this abolition thing too," they warned.

But the women's rights leaders refused to deny Sojourner her chance to speak.

Sojourner listened while one man said that women weren't strong enough to take care of themselves. "Women must be protected," the speaker told the crowd.

Why, I've never been protected in my life, thought Sojourner as she walked up to the speaker's stand. The room was still. Few in the audience had ever seen a black woman dare to address a group.

Sojourner couldn't help thinking about the man who was worried about the protection of women. "The man over there says that women need to be helped into carriages and lifted over ditches, that they should have the best places everywhere. Nobody ever helps me or gives me the best place—and ain't I a woman? I have borne thirteen children and seen most of them sold into slavery, and when I cried out with my mother's grief, none but Jesus heard me—and ain't I a woman?"

The crowd roared approval.

Not everyone who heard Sojourner agreed with her. A man once told her, "I don't care for your talk any more than I do for the bite of a flea."

She replied, "Maybe not, but the Lord willing, I'll keep you scratching."

After the Civil War had started, Sojourner heard about President Lincoln and decided she wanted to see him for herself. In 1864, she met him at the White House. Later, she told her family, "I felt I was with a friend."

However, not everyone in Washington was so friendly. Streetcars, which were the public transportation of the time, were segregated; some were for white people, and some for blacks.

One day Sojourner got tired of waiting for the black car to come along. She got on a white car, and she refused to move when the conductor tried to throw her off.

He hadn't reckoned with Sojourner's will, and he finally gave up and the car began to move.

When Sojourner finished her ride, she noticed that her shoulder hurt. The conductor had yanked on her so hard that it had been dislocated.

To Sojourner, who knew what it was like to fight for what she wanted, her shoulder didn't matter. "Bless God! I've had a ride," she said, grinning.

While she was in Washington, Sojourner met many former slaves who had come from the plantations of the South to live in the city. They didn't know anything about city life, and many of them were no better off than when they were slaves.

Sojourner knew that people had to be free. She thought that if only the black people could go out West, where the land was opening up, they would have a chance to build a good life. She tried to convince the government to help them, but by now, the war was over and people were tired of thinking about the former slaves. Sojourner's plan failed, and many American blacks are still trapped in the cities.

Sojourner died in 1883 in Battle Creek, Michigan, still listening to the voice who had guided her all her life.

Because she believed so strongly that God wanted everyone to be free, Sojourner Truth took enormous risks, and she never turned back.

Mother Jones

"I Shall Stand Firm"

3

Parents kept a close watch on their children as the ship *William*, crowded to the brim with people leaving Ireland, began to pull away from the dock. In 1841, many families were going to America to try to make a better life for themselves.

Mary Harris was eleven years old as she stood on the deck and watched her homeland slip away. In some ways, it was sad to leave the only home she had known, but she was excited, too, about the new adventure. Best of all, she and her brothers and her mother would be with their father again. He had fled Ireland six years earlier to avoid a hangman's noose. Now he had sent them enough money to join him in America.

Although she was on her way to a new life, leaving Ireland behind her, Mary never forgot the poverty of her childhood or the unfair conditions that had caused it. This memory strongly influenced her life.

Mary was born in 1830 in a straw and mud cottage in Ireland. Seeds of revolution were growing among the farmers in County Cork and the rest of the country. The farms were owned by rich landlords, often British, who became even richer while the people who worked the land were barely able to make enough to stay alive. In spite of the unfairness, many landlords continued to raise the rents, and all over Ireland, families were forced out of their homes to wander the roads as they searched for something to eat.

Because their situation was growing so desperate, some of the Irish people turned to violence against the landlords' property. Men took to stealing to get enough food for their families, and Mary's grandfather and father joined in the rebellion.

When she was two years old, Mary's grandfather was arrested and hung. Three years later, her father fled to America to escape the same fate, and now the family was on its way to being together again.

The Harris family settled in Toronto, Canada, where Mary's father worked for the railroad. They were not wealthy, but compared to their life in Ireland, things were much better. There was work for her father, enough food to eat, and many friends.

When Mary was thirteen years old, the first public schools opened in Toronto. They were simple and overcrowded, but Mr. and Mrs. Harris, who themselves had little chance for education, were proud that their children were learning to read and write and do arithmetic. Mary went on to graduate from high school.

Because she wanted to help people, after high school she attended teachers college, called normal school. Because Mary was a Catholic, no one would give her a teaching position, and shortly thereafter, she left Canada. She taught in a convent in Monroe,

Michigan, and finally, at the age of thirty, she became a teacher in Memphis, Tennessee.

There she met George Jones, a young man who worked in a foundry, where hot iron was made into tracks for the railroads that were being built all across the country. Foundry work was hot, hard, and dangerous. The employers were more interested in how much the workers could produce than in the safety of their employees. George tried to interest his fellow workers in joining a new union to better their conditions, but he had little success, for most of them thought the cause was hopeless. They knew the company would not give up any of its power without a struggle.

In 1860, the Civil War threatened, and that same year Mary Harris and George Jones were married. When the war reached Memphis, life in the city was confusing and very sad as local sons and husbands went off to fight. For the newlyweds, the sadness was mixed with joy, for in 1862 their first baby was born. By the end of the war, in 1865, they had three more children.

Once the war was over, business began to boom. George was able to interest workers in union organizing again, and this time he was more successful. The Memphis local of the Iron Molders Union was founded.

George traveled the area organizing for the union. Mary was glad for him and took a great interest in what he was doing. They both believed that working people needed the support of unions to better their lives.

George and Mary had each other, their family, and their pride in the new union. But just when the future was looking bright, another tragedy struck Memphis, which was only beginning to recover from the war years. In 1867, a yellow fever epidemic began and spread quickly. Doctors tried all kinds of cures, but since it had not yet been discovered that mosquitoes carried the disease, their work was of little use.

Within two weeks, all four of George and Mary Harris Jones's children were dead. A few days later, George died too.

Mary had left her home in Ireland; she had left her family in Canada. Now her husband and children were gone, and she prayed she would die with them.

But Mary Jones did not die, and soon she was helping other families. When the epidemic was finally over, Mary wanted to leave Memphis behind. The men of the Iron Molders Union gave her what money they could spare, and she moved to Chicago, got work as a seamstress, and tried to begin a new life.

Chicago was growing fast. Many businessmen had become millionaires. America seemed to be entering a period of wealth, and some people thought this meant that God preferred the rich. John D. Rockefeller, Jr., one of the richest men in the country, said, "I believe that the power to make money is the gift of God."

In the meantime, the people of the working class continued to be poor.

Some people believed that poverty was God's

34

punishment for sins. If a businessman believed this way, he was not likely to be concerned with the working conditions for his employees or with their children, who were often ill and hungry.

Chicago was crowded with both rich and poor, and although Mary was able to earn enough money for herself by sewing clothes for rich women, she could not forget the bad conditions that existed for most of the people.

Mary had been in Chicago less than a year when the Great Chicago Fire, as it came to be called, struck the city and burned for three days. When it was over, one-sixth of the city was destroyed.

As usual, it was the poor who suffered most.

Once again, instead of giving up, Mary Jones helped the people. During this period, she met members of the Knights of Labor, a secret organization that was trying to improve working conditions, and it was among the people of this group that Mary at last found a place to belong. She began traveling and speaking, trying to get working people to join unions. If enough people did this, she believed, they would gain power, and then their employers, as well as the government, would have to listen to their demands.

Although many women worked outside of their homes, few were political leaders, or even active in social concerns. Many people thought that women should be quiet and polite. "Be a lady," parents told their daughters.

Mary didn't agree. "A lady is the last thing on earth I want to be," she roared, for she believed that women, as well as men, could change the world.

She talked to women workers and to the wives of

strikers. "Fight like hell whatever your fight. For God's sake, don't be ladylike" was her motto. She had seen too much misery and death to waste time on false modesty and manners.

In 1877 the Pennsylvania Railroad and other industrial giants cut the wages of workers, but not the profits (the amount of money made by the owners). A railroad strike began that quickly grew into a conflict between labor on one side and big business and government, which sent troops in to protect the railroad property, on the other.

In Pittsburgh, Pennsylvania, twenty-six people, including children, were killed when the soldiers fired on the crowd. The laborers were helpless against that kind of power, and that was the end of the strike.

The workers had lost. The men went back to work for the same low wages. But one good thing happened. For the first time, workers had seen that they could organize and that many townspeople were on their side.

Mary was in Pittsburgh at the time of the strike. Until then, she had agreed with the Knights of Labor, who believed that working conditions could change for the better without strikes, just by employers and workers talking to each other. After what happened with the railroads, Mary knew better.

She left the Knights of Labor and began traveling around the country, going wherever she was needed. People began to call her Mother Jones because she cared for the people as much as she had loved the children she had lost.

In 1891, she went to Virginia when the miners

there were fired because they joined the new United Mine Workers Union. Coal mining was an extraordinarily dangerous occupation, and the pay was usually low.

The people lived together in "company towns" where the mine owners controlled the lives of the workers. Sometimes the miners were paid in coupons, called *scrip*, instead of in cash. These coupons could only be cashed at the company store, where the mine owners charged the laborers far too much for food and other necessities. The miners were even told what books they could read. Their life was hard; their pleasures few.

The miners finally had enough bad treatment and they decided to strike. Mary Jones led a meeting on the highway, for no one would rent her a hall. She once gave her speech standing in the middle of a creek because she would have been arrested for trespassing on company property had she stood on dry land on either side. She was sixty-one years old now. This strike was lost, but others were won, and slowly, the miners began to make gains.

Mother Jones could have rested, but she began hearing more and more about another serious problem in America: children as young as six years old were working in factories for eight hours every day and earning about ten cents a day.

Worse than the hours and the pay were the accidents. Because they were children, they were forced to do dangerous jobs that adults would have refused, and they were often so tired that they fell asleep at their machines. Many were injured or killed.

At first, Mary could not believe this was happening. She began to work in factories to find out for herself, and what she saw made her so mad that, for once, she felt helpless. "I had to leave there," she said. "I'd rather be with the coal miners or in the mining camps where the labor fight was at least being fought by grown men."

Mary had seen her own children die, but this was different. Businessmen were making profit from the suffering of children. She felt that she wasn't strong enough to fight this fight.

For a while Mary worked in West Virginia with the coal miners, and she would tell miners and their families, "This is God's work. He wants men to organize and come out of the land of slavery into the land of freedom."

She never had much use for the mine owners who abused the workers and then went to church on Sunday and considered themselves holy. Now in her seventies, white-haired, her blue eyes gleaming, Mary would protest that "the owners cheat and starve the workers all week and then give money to the church on Sunday. Jesus never wanted that."

She was also sure that God never intended for children, rich or poor, to be treated as slaves. Mother Jones had never forgotten the children in the factories, and in 1903 she organized the Children's Crusade in which some two hundred child laborers between the ages of eight and ten marched ninety miles from Philadelphia to New York in an effort to make America see what was happening. To the people along the way, the children held up their hands, with fingers missing from accidents, and they told how they spent their days. Although President Teddy Roosevelt, who was vacationing in New York at the time, refused to see the children, the march was not a failure. The people who saw them, as well as the children themselves, began to understand that changes must be made.

For the rest of her life, Mary Jones spent her time helping working people. She never gave up. Often, without legitimate charges, she found herself in jail, and she wrote, "To be shut away from the sunlight is not pleasant, but I shall stand firm. To be in prison is no disgrace."

Mary died in 1930 at the age of one hundred.

It is said that Jesus came to comfort the afflicted and to afflict the comforted. In her own way, Mary Harris Jones did the same.

Mother Jones spent her long life trying to bring justice where there was injustice. She often lost her fights, but she never stopped trying. The improved conditions for workingmen and women—and the laws that protect children today—are possible because people like Mary Harris Jones cared enough to begin the fight.

Corrie
ten Boom

"We Must Tell People"

4

For the first fifty years of her life, when Corrie ten Boom woke up each morning, she knew exactly how the day would go. It was always the same: breakfast with her family, then Scripture reading, then a day's work in the family watch-repair shop. Some people would have found such daily repetition boring, but to Corrie, it was perfect.

She had lived in the same house since she was born, and even now she says, "I would have been content to spend all my days there."

But all the security of that routine changed when World War II came to Holland. Before the war ended, Corrie ten Boom became a prisoner in the dreaded Ravensbrück concentration camp in Germany. Now she travels all over the world telling people about that experience, but the story she tells is not one of sadness and despair. It is full of the hope that she found even as danger and death surrounded her.

One of Corrie's earliest memories is of her father reading Scripture at breakfast. When she was born on April 15, 1892, in Haarlem, the Netherlands, the Ten Boom Watch Shop had already been in the family for fifty-five years. Each day of Corrie's life began with the members of her family and all employees of the shop gathering around the table to listen to Mr. ten Boom read from the old black Bible.

Life was calm and well organized. While Corrie and her brother and sisters played around the house, her father would go to his workbench. Mrs. ten Boom spent much time helping the poor of Haarlem, and the Ten Boom house was always full of company.

Several of Corrie's aunts lived with them. One was Tante Bep, who was always complaining. No matter what happened, Tante Bep found some way to find fault.

One day Corrie asked her mother why her aunt was so grouchy all the time. "Is there something I could do, mama, that would make her smile, just for a little while?"

Mama laughed and said, "Tante Bep would be unhappy no matter what you did because she's never learned the secret. Happiness isn't something that depends on our surroundings, Corrie. It's something we make inside ourselves."

Corrie spent her childhood in this happy household, and when she was in her early twenties, she fell in love with Karel, who was a young minister, a friend of her brother Willem. But Karel's family disapproved because they felt that the daughter of a watchmaker wasn't a suitable match for their son, and he sadly said good-bye to Corrie.

After she recovered from this disappointment, Corrie settled into the routine that she was to follow for the next twenty years, never dreaming of the drama in store for her. After she finished high school, Corrie became the first licensed woman watchmaker in Holland, and her life seemed set.

To Corrie, it was the perfect life. She was a little shy and had never thought of leaving home. Here, surrounded by people she loved, she reached her forty-eighth birthday.

But the world outside her shop was changing, and soon her family's life would change too. For months, the family had listened to the radio reports as the Germans advanced across Europe, and in May 1940, the German airplanes bombed Holland for five days and nights. When the noise stopped, the little country had surrendered. World War II had come to Holland.

From the very first night of the fighting, Corrie began to wonder how she and her family would be affected by the war. She had a dream that first night that troubled her greatly. As she tried to sleep, she had a vision of herself and some of her family and friends being pulled through the streets of Haarlem in a wagon. No matter how hard they tried, they couldn't get off. Later, Corrie was to remember this dream.

At first, the German occupation didn't make much difference to Corrie. Although soldiers were in the streets and in the shops now, the family continued as before, with one important exception.

Each night, Corrie and her family listened to radio broadcasts from England. This was strictly forbidden, as all private radios were against the law. The newspapers printed only news that made Germany look strong. As the Ten Booms listened to the BBC from London, they learned the truth about how the war was going. They learned that the Nazis were killing many Jews.

The Ten Booms were strong members of the Dutch Reformed Church, but they had many friends and customers who were Jewish. The Nazis' hatred of these people crossed into Holland with the war, and Corrie and her family were ashamed at how many of the Dutch went along with the looting and burning of Jewish homes and synagogues.

Signs began to pop up everywhere that said No Jews, or Jews Not Wanted Here, and every Jew, young or old, was forced to wear a six-pointed yellow star on her or his clothing. The word *Jood* marked the wearer as an outcast. As friends and acquaintances began to disappear, the Ten Booms hoped that some had managed to escape, but they knew that the Gestapo, the Nazi secret police, were arresting more people every day.

One day Corrie and her father saw a truck loaded with Jewish men, women, and children who were being taken away.

"Those poor people!" Corrie cried.

"Yes, those poor people," her father agreed. But he was watching the soldiers, and he felt sorry for them too. This war was bad for everyone.

The Ten Boom family had always helped anyone in need. Now, they made the decision that they would help the Jews, although this would not be as safe as helping a sick neighbor. In helping to save the lives of others, the Ten Booms were risking their own.

Soon enough, their chance came to help. Mr. Weil, who owned the fur shop across the street, needed to escape quickly. The Germans had broken into his shop and taken all of his merchandise. He knew they would come back to arrest him. He had committed no crime. He was Jewish, and that was reason enough in wartime Holland.

With the aid of her brother Willem, who was a pastor in a country church, Corrie found Mr. Weil a safe place of escape.

A few weeks later, a woman came to the Ten Booms' doors in the night. "I am a Jew, and I must get away from the Nazis. Can I come in?" she asked fearfully.

The Ten Booms were just getting ready to have tea. As if it were the most natural thing in the world, Corrie invited the woman to join them.

She had come because the Jews of Haarlem had heard of how the Ten Booms had helped Mr. Weil. "Could you let me stay just a little while?" Mrs. Kleemaker was so afraid.

Father answered, "In this household, God's people are always welcome."

Other Jews began coming to the house, seeking shelter. The Ten Boom house was only a half a block from the main police headquarters, and in order to keep their Jewish guests safe when the soldiers searched the houses, the Ten Booms built a secret room that would serve as a hiding place until escape from the city could be arranged.

The man who built the room for them was happy and proud of the job he had done. "The Gestapo could search for a year," he said. "They'll never find this one."

Over the next months, a constant stream of Jews

passed through the house, grateful for the Ten Booms' loving care. Whenever danger seemed near, they would dash to the secret place.

The Ten Booms thought that the work they were doing was holy. When people warned them that they shouldn't get involved—"Why risk your lives for a Jew?"—Father ten Boom answered for the whole family. "You say we could lose our lives for this work. I would consider that the greatest honor that could come to my family."

For a while, their work continued. One day, however, time ran out. On February 28, 1944, the Germans raided the Ten Boom house. Corrie and her sisters Betsie and Nollie, her brother Willem, her nephew Peter, her father, and twenty-nine others were arrested and taken to jail. The secret room was never discovered, and the Jews who had hidden there were safe.

As the family was taken away by the police, Corrie suddenly remembered the dream she had dreamed on the first night of the war. It had come true. They were being taken where they would not go. Corrie was fifty-three years old. Her secure world in the watch shop had vanished forever.

First they were sent to a prison in Holland. Corrie, who had spoken up to protect her father, was known as the ringleader, and she was put into solitary confinement. A kind nurse managed to smuggle a copy of the Gospels in to her, and as she sat all alone in her cell and read the Scripture over and over, she began to wonder how to take this horrible situation and turn it to good.

Her father, an old man, died after nine days in the prison. Soon the rest of the family, except for Corrie and Betsie, were released.

Shortly after this, the prisoners learned that the Allied invasion that was to free Holland had begun. Corrie rejoiced for her country. But for the prisoners themselves, the news meant something different from freedom. The prison was evacuated and on June 5, 1944, they were moved deeper into German-held territory. The Germans would not let the prisoners go free.

Corrie was sent to a concentration camp that the Germans had built to hold the many people, Jews and Christians alike, whom they had arrested. Betsie was assigned to the same camp, and they thanked God over and over again for being together.

Just as they had all their lives, Betsie and Corrie prayed together. As well as praying for the prisoners, they began to ask God to help the soldiers and prison officials to have a change of heart. Their journey of forgiveness had begun.

Once again, Corrie and Betsie were transferred. This time the train took them inside Germany itself, and as they read the name on the gate of this new place, their hearts grew cold with fear.

It was the women's camp at Ravensbruck. Even back in Haarlem, people had heard of this concentration camp where women were crowded together in filth and misery. All night long they could hear the screams of people being tortured.

Worst of all, in the middle of the camp was a smokestack with gray smoke coming out in a constant flow. This was the crematorium, the ovens where the bodies of the thousands of prisoners were burned.

And yet, in the midst of this unthinkable horror, Corrie and Betsie found a new kind of peace. All their lives they had listened to their father as he read the Bible to them, and now the words had new meaning. The Scripture came to life as Corrie read again and again of how Jesus had been arrested and beaten. It reminded the women of their own lives in Ravensbrück.

Betsie, especially, lived the words of Jesus—"Forgive them, Father, for they know not what they do"—as she continued to pray for the Germans. Betsie was planning for the future.

"When this is over, we must tell people, Corrie," Betsie would say. "We must tell them what we learned—that no matter how bad things get, Jesus is still with us."

During the day, the women worked in the factories of Ravensbrück. At night, even if they were exhausted, Corrie and Betsie took out their Bible. Soon other women were praying in the crowded barracks, and in this place of death there came a small ray of light.

The camp officials just laughed. "Have you heard about barracks 28? It's the crazy place, where they still hope."

Even in a concentration camp, Betsie and Corrie were saving people as they had been taught to do. Corrie's faith was to be tested, however. Betsie, worn out by the hard prison life, died as 1944 came to an end. Her spirit was as strong as ever, but her body could go on no longer.

Just a few days later, on December 28, 1944, Corrie was released from Ravensbrück. One week later, all the women in her age-group were killed. She wondered if God had spared her for a reason.

Corrie returned to Holland, to the house of her childhood. Her father and Betsie were dead, but most of her family was there to greet her.

Surely now she could rest. Prison had been a terrible ordeal. For a while she tried working in the watch shop again, but before long, she grew restless. As she worked, Corrie could hear Betsie urging, "We must tell people."

So, at the age of fifty-three years, Corrie began spreading the message of forgiveness. First she spoke to the people of Holland. As the war ended and more and more prisoners came home, Corrie noticed that the ones who got well again were those who were able to forgive the Germans who had hurt them so deeply.

From Holland, Corrie began to travel all over the world telling people of her experience in the concentration camp. More important than the suffering, she would explain, was the discovery that God is always with us, even in a hell like Ravensbrück. She urged people never to give up on life and always to forgive those who hurt them.

Corrie doesn't pretend to understand the reason for all that has happened to her.

"Life is like embroidery," she says. "The bottom side, the part that we can see, is knotted and tangled up. But if we could look at it from the right side, we would see that God is making a design of great beauty."

49

Jeannette Piccard

The Seventy-Year Dream

5.

It was bedtime, and Jeannette's mother came into her room to tuck her in. Tonight, her mother sat down on the bed and looked at her. "You know, darling, it seems like yesterday when you were a baby, and here you are, eleven years old. You're starting to grow up now. Have you ever thought about what you want to do with your life?"

Mother's face was so sweet as she sat there in the moonlight. How could Jeannette tell her mother the truth when she could barely understand it herself? But there was no turning back from her decision.

"Mother, I want to be a priest."

"A priest?" was all her mother could stammer as she burst into tears and ran from the room. The year was 1906, and nice Episcopalian girls did not think such things.

Where could Jeannette have gotten such an outlandish idea in the first place? Certainly not from seeing women priests in her own church, for there weren't any. Women weren't on the altar at all. Even if they sang in the choir, they were kept out of sight, in their places behind the organ. In 1906, ladies were not seen in the church in any public role.

Many years later, when Jeannette Ridlon Piccard

became one of the first women priests of the Episcopal Church in the United States, she was to remember that night of her childhood and her mother's reaction. "I still feel sorry for poor mother. She probably thought I'd say I wanted to get married and have children. Well, I did do that. It's just that I had other things to do, too. I always wanted to be a priest, as long as I can remember. In churchy language, you could say I felt called to priesthood. To me, that means that God wanted me to do this, and then I wanted it too."

Almost seventy years would pass between that night with her mother and Jeannette's ordination in 1974. But during those years, Jeannette Piccard did not simply sit around and wait. She has had a full, exciting life.

Jeannette was born an identical twin in 1895. She and her sister were so alike that people could only tell them apart because Jeannette had a mole on her right wrist. One day, when they were three years old, her sister accidentally set herself on fire and died, and two years later another sister died of appendicitis. In those days, there were no antibiotics to reduce infection, and the operation for the appendix was very serious.

"I was aware of pain and death through the loss of these two sisters," Jeannette recalls, "but for the most part, I've seen so little of life firsthand. I've been surrounded all my life by ladies and gentlemen. We never had to live in misery or poverty. Both of my parents were honest and loving and kind."

It was from this gentle background that Jeannette entered Bryn Mawr College in 1914.

The college president met with each freshman to ask her about herself, and when she asked Jeannette what she wanted to be after graduation, Jeannette answered in the same way as she had answered her mother years before. "I want something impossible, I want to be a priest of the Episcopal Church."

This time the reaction was different. The president smiled and said, "Oh, my dear, by the time you graduate, that may be entirely possible."

Jeannette was relieved and happy to receive such support. However, the Bryn Mawr president was wrong. Ordination in the priesthood for women was not to come until 1974, and then only under difficult conditions.

In college, Jeannette studied science and education. In some ways, she felt she was leading two different lives. In one, she was preparing for an acceptable career, and in the other she was clinging to her dream.

"I kept wanting and responding to the call, but at the same time I accepted that it was impossible," says Jeannette. "I never quit talking about it, yet I never believed it would happen."

After graduating from Bryn Mawr, she went to the University of Chicago where she got a master's degree in chemistry, and it was here that she met someone she would change the course of her life.

He was one of her professors. When Jeannette first saw Jean Piccard, her first impression was of a thin, unattractive man, but as she got to know him better, the two found they had a great deal in common, and the following summer, in 1919, they were married.

Jean was also one of twins. He and his brother Auguste were inventors and scientists. In 1905, when they were thirteen, an aunt had given them a copy of Jules Verne's *Twenty Thousand Leagues Under the Sea,* and they had been so fascinated that they quickly designed a bathyscaphe of their own to use for exploring deep-sea waters.

Jeannette and Jean were both adventurous and unafraid of exploring new territory. Because her husband needed a pilot for an experiment with helium passenger balloons, Jeannette got her balloon pilot's license.

"He needed someone that he could trust and depend on," Jeannette explained. "In a marriage, you help each other. If I needed someone to change diapers, he did that. We helped each other all we could."

Before she could get her balloon license, however, Jeannette had to make a solo flight at night. But she never hesitated to attempt new skills, so, all alone, she climbed into an old much-mended balloon that was called *Patches* because of all the repairs it had received.

Jeannette obtained her license, and she was ready to join her husband and Auguste in a historic experiment. They were going to attempt to fly up into the stratosphere—the upper part of the earth's atmosphere. They took off at seven in the morning in Dearborn, Michigan, and when they landed at three that afternoon in Cadiz, Ohio, they had gone almost ten miles straight up into the air, setting a new world's record. Except for the flight of the Russian astronaut Valentina Tereshkova in 1963, no woman has gone as far above the earth's surface.

The Piccards won many awards for their work. Over the years, Jeannette made more flights, and although she enjoyed working with her husband and her brother-in-law, she never forgot her early dream.

"I enjoyed the work," she says, "but my vocation was always to the priesthood, not to science."

Still, her dream seemed destined to remain just that. The years passed and the Episcopal Church did not change its stand that only men could become priests.

Jeannette knew the story of the talents that is told in the Bible. God gives many talents, or gifts, to everyone. But they are meant to be used. What was she to do with this talent that no one would let her use publicly? "I knew that God wanted me to do what I could, in whatever way I could, until the time came when I was allowed to be a priest."

Finally, after so many years of waiting, it seemed as though the world of the Episcopal Church was about to change. The structure of the Episcopal Church consists of the laity, the deacons, the priests, and the bishops. In 1971, the Church took a new position. Women could become ordained deacons. Until that year, women had not been allowed to join this order, whose members performed some sacramental duties.

"The Church had allowed a woman to be a deaconess for years. But that was a horse of a different color! A deacon could administer the sacraments and take Communion to the sick. A deaconess was expected to visit the sick, but she was never allowed to administer Communion. Women just weren't supposed to be doing that kind of thing."

Throughout the years, Jeannette had continued to talk to clergy and other people about her desire to become a priest. This desire, she felt, was based on the sound theological basis of the sacrament of baptism.

"One baptized Christian is the equal of any other baptized Christian, male or female. I've always felt that way." Jeannette would try to persuade her listeners. "Others don't agree with me. They say that, yes, anyone can be baptized, but then equality stops. Only men have the chance to become priests."

Jeannette was ordained a deacon in December 1971. Some deacons remained as members of that order, but many others went on to become priests. This is what Jeannette had always felt called to do, and although the Church still did not support her dream, she completed the same educational requirements as those men who would go on to become priests.

In 1973, Jeannette fully expected her time to come. In the Episcopal Church, a group called the General Convention is the governing body that has the authority to decide such questions as whether women can become priests. That year, the convention met in Kentucky, and Jeannette anxiously awaited their verdict. Nothing in the canon, or law, of the Church especially forbade women priests, but neither did anything say they could exist. Surely now was the time for the convention to speak out, loud and clear.

The men of the convention spoke out. But what they said was no. After such a disappointment, some of the people who believed in women's ordination decided that they must take action on their own.

In July 1974, Jeannette's phone rang. It was Sue Hiatt, another of the women who wanted to become a priest. "We've found three bishops who have agreed to ordain qualified women," she said. "Jeannette, do you want to be included?"

"Certainly," came the reply. For Jeannette, there was no doubt. "Certainly."

"Stop and think. This is a serious step." Sue wanted to make sure Jeannette realized what she was doing. "There may be trouble."

What they were planning to do had not been formally approved by the governing body of their Church. Although some people in the Church would support their act, others would condemn them as rebels.

"Well, Sue, for fifty years I've been saying that if I could find a bishop anywhere who would do it, I would be ordained. Of course I'm coming."

As word spread of what the women were planning to do, opposition to their plan was growing.

"How can you do something like this?" people asked Jeannette. "We've never done it that way before. You're going against tradition."

Jeannette just smiled and quoted Tertullian, a

Christian from the second century. "Jesus said 'I am Truth,' he did not say 'I am tradition.' Therefore, we can change tradition."

On July 29, 1974, Jeannette Piccard and ten other women were ordained priests of the Episcopal Church. One of the women was twenty-seven years old. Jeannette, at seventy-nine, was the oldest.

"This was the most important moment of my life," says Jeannette. "It's really impossible to describe. People tell me that I looked as radiant and beautiful as any young bride or groom."

Jeannette's three sons took part in the ceremony, and her many friends shared her happiness. Not all Episcopalians were as kind. Some thought that the eleven women had performed an act of rebellion against Church authority. Her own bishop forbade her to act as a priest in his diocese. After all the years of waiting, Jeannette had been ordained, and yet she was not allowed to function as a priest.

The eleven women weren't the only ones to find themselves in trouble. The three bishops who had ordained them were criticized, and so were the priests who allowed the women to give sermons at their churches.

For a while after the ordination, Jeannette felt like an outcast. "Some people still cannot accept the fact that a woman is a person." However, as time went on, she found that those who opposed her continued to do so, but others came to accept her and the other women.

Why is it so hard for people to think of women as priests? Jeannette has given this question considerable thought. "The idea of a priest being only male comes from the time of the Dark Ages. If people would only read Genesis in the Bible, it says there that God created people, male and female. He created them in his own image. But people today still think that only men can represent God, as if God were a male. But God is Everything.

"And too many people have forgotten that a priest should be the servant, not the boss, of the people. Not all priests are like this, but some are.

"I think the most important thing for me to do as a priest is to tell people that God loves them and that Jesus came to show this love."

Jeannette glows as she talks about her ministry.

In 1977, Jeannette Piccard was recognized by the Episcopal Church as a priest in good standing in the Diocese of Minnesota. She had waited for almost seventy years to be ordained. Now she has a granddaughter who is an Episcopal priest, too.

Jeannette serves as a good example of someone who had a dream and was faithful to it. She put her other gifts to use while she was waiting, and she never grew bitter.

Throughout her life, Jeannette has forged new pathways, whether in the stratosphere or in the Church. And she never let her dream die.

Dorothy Day

"Like Someone's Grandma"

6.

If you found yourself all alone in a city today, with no money, or friends, or place to rest, what could you do? In over fifty cities in America, you could go to a place called a Catholic Worker house, and you would be welcomed.

The first House of Hospitality, as they are called, was started in New York City in 1933 by Dorothy Day. Until her death (November 29, 1980), she lived in New York City, surrounded by friends in the Catholic Worker movement she helped found.

When Dorothy Day was born in New York in 1897, there was little reason to guess where her life would lead. Dorothy was the third of five children. Her parents had been baptized, but they were not particularly interested in going to church. The Days had a maid named Mary who was Catholic, and she once took the young Dorothy along to mass with her. Dorothy remembers the event: "Mary was so embarrassed that she never took me back. She told my parents that all I wanted to do was climb up on the pew and look around."

Dorothy's father, John Day, was a newspaperman, and at the time of the San Francisco earthquake of 1906, she and her family were living in California.

As well as the destruction and huge losses suffered by people, Dorothy saw something that was to remain with her for the rest of her life. "In the middle of all their heartaches," she wrote years later, "I saw people helping each other. It was here that I learned the joy of doing good and sharing with others."

The Day family moved to Chicago shortly after the earthquake. John and Grace Day had a baby boy, who was named after his father. Dorothy loved to put baby John into his carriage and push him all around the neighborhood.

Her older brother Donald had begun to work for a newspaper that reported on the condition of the workingmen and women in Chicago. Life was very hard, especially for the immigrants who had just come to America.

Dorothy began to wonder about the people she read about in her brother's newspaper. As she walked with the baby carriage, she wandered around Chicago's West Side, where many of the working-class people lived. As she got to know them, she saw that, no matter how hard they worked, they were not able to move ahead in this new country.

Dorothy tried to think of ways to help these people. She joined the Episcopal Church and began to read and pray. Perhaps she would find answers in religion. This was the beginning of her search for a way to help the poor.

After high school, Dorothy won a scholarship to the University of Illinois. It was exciting for her to be around people who were interested in the same things that she cared so much about.

Surely, she thought, if enough people cared, something could be done. Dorothy began to realize that many churchgoers didn't seem to want to do anything concrete to help others. They were satisfied singing hymns and going to church and just talking about helping people, instead of working to change things.

This was a sad time in Dorothy's life. She gave up both the Church and the God whom she had loved. All around her were the poor and their problems. Without her belief in God, Dorothy felt terribly lonely.

When her family moved to New York City, Dorothy was shocked by the conditions there. Chicago had seemed bad enough. New York was worse by far. Besides being crowded, it was so much dirtier, and everywhere she went, Dorothy saw men without homes, families without food.

Most people would have decided that they alone couldn't improve things, and they would have tried to forget what they saw.

Not Dorothy. For her, the only question was, how to help.

She started by being a reporter for a newspaper named *Call*, and working there, she met many men and women who wanted to help the poor as much as she did. It was an exciting period in American history. Labor unions were just getting started. Different political parties were trying to change conditions.

It was 1919, and another issue was being debated in American society: the question of whether or not women should be allowed to vote. That year, Dorothy joined a group of women who hoped to change people's minds and hurry the day when both women and men would have the right to vote. They picketed the White House in Washington, D.C., and what happened instead was that Dorothy and the others were arrested and sentenced to thirty days in jail.

During those days in prison, Dorothy had a lot of time to think. Added to her support for women's rights was a new vision of prison reform, but she felt frustrated in her desire to make life better. Somehow, in the midst of this sadness, she remembered the years when she had believed in God, and she picked up a Bible and read "They that sow in tears will reap in joy."

Dorothy wondered whether she would ever be happy again.

Soon after this experience, she and the others were released from jail.

In the days that followed her release, Dorothy threw herself into finding answers to the problems that she saw. Before long, she had forgotten God once more.

In 1925, she fell in love with a man named Forster Batterham. They wanted to live together. Forster was an atheist. He didn't believe in God and saw no need to be involved with any church.

For a while, their life together was happy. Forster was a biologist, Dorothy continued her writing, and they spent hours studying nature or looking at the stars.

Dorothy had never been so contented. Gradually, she found herself praying again. No world this wonderful could happen by accident, she thought. There has to be a Creator.

She only wished that Forster could share her faith in God, and more and more they grew apart. When their daughter, Tamar, was born in 1927, it was evident that they could not stay together much longer. Forster looked at the world and saw only ugliness, he had not wanted to bring a child into it.

Dorothy was filled with joy when she looked at Tamar. She wanted her baby to have more meaning in her life than she herself had found, and she decided that Tamar should be baptized in the Catholic Church.

Forster did not agree. When Dorothy became a Catholic, too, she felt she had made a choice. She had had to decide who would be more important in her life, Forster or God, and as much as she loved Forster, she had to leave him. Dorothy knew she had done the right thing, but that didn't make the pain stop hurting.

As she learned more about her new religion, Dorothy began asking serious questions. Why wasn't the Catholic Church helping more? The church sometimes gave food or clothing to the poor, but the people who seemed to be doing the most to change the conditions that caused poverty in the first place didn't belong to any church. This was the time of the Great Depression in America. In the early 1930s, many people were without jobs and without hope. If only the churches would use their power to help, something good might begin to happen.

Then Dorothy decided not to wait any longer for

the church to do something. She prayed that God would show her what he wanted her to do. "I realized that the people who belong to a church should go ahead and quit waiting to be told what to do. You don't need permission to perform the works of mercy. We all can do something, and doing that will lead to something else."

One day, there was a knock at her door. She didn't know it yet, but her prayers had been answered. At last, Dorothy would begin to help the poor in a concrete way.

The man at the door was named Peter Maurin. He had spent years thinking about the poor, and a friend of his had told him about Dorothy. Now he had a plan to share with her.

There were three main points to his idea. The first was to begin a newspaper, in order to get people thinking. Next, he wanted to open "a house of hospitality," that would be a place where anyone could come and be welcomed. Because he believed that city life made it harder for people to be good, he also wanted to organize some farm communities.

Dorothy wasn't too sure about the house and the farms, but she did know how to write.

"But where will we get the money?" she asked Peter.

He shrugged. "People are what's important. The money will come. God won't forget us."

The money did come, and on May 1, 1933, the first copy of the newspaper was ready. It was called the *Catholic Worker*.

The newspaper came as a surprise to many. At

last people who said they believed in God were starting to try to help. Maybe the poor had a friend.

The *Catholic Worker* was much more of a success than Dorothy and Peter had dreamed. People began coming to their door. Some asked for help, but many also wanted to know how they could help. The second part of Peter's plan, the Houses of Hospitality, began. The Catholic Workers, as Dorothy and the others were now being called, started a soup kitchen and opened a place for homeless people to stay.

Soon there was enough money to buy a small farm, and Peter Maurin was happy to see all three parts of his plan begin to take shape.

Now that the *Catholic Worker* was on its feet, Dorothy was able to spend a little more time on her other concerns. She supported a group of workers who were trying to start a union. Some people, who had approved of the newspaper, the hospitality house, and the farm, were against Catholic Workers getting involved in labor struggles.

"The church should stay out of politics," people told her. "Just do religious work and leave the rest alone."

Dorothy believed that working for justice and peace were what the message of Jesus was about.

One of the most severe tests of her belief came during World War II. To Dorothy, there was no way a person could support a war if she or he didn't believe in violence—even if it were a war that seemed necessary in the defense of America. During a time of great patriotism, Dorothy and other pacifists—

people who refused to use violence—were heavily criticized for taking this stand.

When the atomic bomb was dropped on Hiroshima and Nagasaki, the war with Japan was quickly ended. Dorothy was horrified that so many innocent people had died, and this was the beginning of her fight against nuclear weapons, which continues to this day.

By the end of World War II, Houses of Hospitality were beginning to spread across the country. More and more people were trying to live as Peter Maurin and Dorothy Day had shown them.

After the war, Dorothy turned her attention to the civil rights movement. Years before, she had wondered why the Church didn't speak out for the poor. Now she tried to stir the indifferent Christians of the 1950s into action. There was much work to be done before black women, men, and children would have a fair chance at a good life.

In the 1970s, Dorothy joined the struggle of the United Farm Workers. The people who labor in the fields picking lettuce, grapes, and other foods were at the mercy of the farmers, and Dorothy wanted to help them form a union of their own. At the age of seventy-five, Dorothy Day was arrested on the picket line. It was the eighth time she had been in a jail because of her concern for others.

Many people come to New York to see Dorothy Day. Sometimes they were disappointed.

If they were expecting to see someone who looked different from or holier than other people, they were surprised. She led an exciting life, but it was also very ordinary. She lived in poverty, and one of her chief joys was playing with her grandchildren.

People often left shaking their heads. "Why, she looks just like someone's grandma," they said, as if that meant she was helpless.

The important thing about Dorothy Day's life is not how she looked. What matters is what she did. Even when she was many years and many miles away from the San Francisco earthquake, where she saw people helping each other, the words she spoke still held true. "I saw the joy of doing good and sharing with others."

Catherine
de Hueck
Doherty

"A Living Flame"

7

The trees gently waved in the morning breeze as Catherine stood looking out the door of the hut where she had spent the night in prayer. In the language of her childhood, this hut, a special place, was called a *poustinia*. Although she had been in Canada for many years now, she still thought often of her native Russia. She remembered so much of the land, the people, and the hermits she had known. It was from them that she had gotten the ideas for so much that had become part of her life here in Ontario.

In Russia, it was a centuries-old tradition that some people would feel called to give away all they had and go off to live in the woods or some other deserted place. There they would pray to God, and they would be available to help whoever came to see them.

A *poustinik*, or "hermit," had lived near Catherine's house, and her mother would often take Catherine with her and go to him to ask for advice.

"I never knew his name," Catherine remembers, "but I always felt welcome there. He was a joyful person. After he had shared tea with us, I would run outside to play, and he and my mother would discuss whatever it was that bothered her."

Aside from listening to people and giving advice, a *poustinik* also was available to people who asked for help. If a farmer went to him and asked for help with the crops because a storm was on the way, the *poustinik* would be there.

When a man decided to become a *poustinik*, he settled his affairs and went off quietly to begin his new life. Once, a friend of Catherine's father became one of these hermits.

"His name was Peter, and he was very rich. After praying a long time, he decided to give away all of his money, and he went through the slums of the city of Petrograd passing out pieces of silver and gold. Then he went home, put on a long robe, took with him only bread, water, salt and a walking stick, and left. It was the last my father saw of his friend for a long time."

Many years later, Catherine's father was coming out of a church when he recognized one of the beggars on the steps of the building. It was his friend Peter, as poor as he had ever been rich, but very happy. He had spent the years serving others and praying.

Catherine's life had been surrounded with such people. She was born on the Feast of the Assumption, August 15, 1900, and from the beginning, her life was full of religious influence.

Her mother's name had been Emma Thompson. Her father was Theodore de Kolyschkine, an officer in the army of the czar, Alexander II. Her father was half Polish and a Catholic. His daughter was baptized into the same religion, but because there was no Catholic church within ninety miles, Catherine was raised in the Russian Orthodox tradition, which emphasized the mercy of God, and the presence of Christ in a special way in the poor.

The Kolyschkines were a wealthy family, but even though there were many servants, Catherine was taught to do all sorts of work around the house and the estate.

All at once, her father lost most of his money in an unfortunate business deal. The family had to move to simple quarters and let most of the servants go.

"I thought it was great fun to be poor," Catherine laughs now. "Luckily, father began making money again before I had time to learn that the fun of poverty quickly runs out."

Because of her father's army career, the family moved about a great deal. Catherine lived in Egypt for a time, and she went to school in France. But, her love for Russia always remained strong. She couldn't imagine that a time might come when she would not be welcome to live in her beloved country.

When Catherine was fifteen years old, she married the Baron Boris de Hueck. She moved from her family's house to the equally elegant house of her new husband, but by the next year, events in the world would begin to change her life forever.

In 1916 Boris went off to war, and Catherine decided to become a Red Cross nurse. Russia was fighting the Germans in World War I. As the fighting against outsiders ended, Russia faced another threat: a revolution had begun.

For years the czar and the rich noble families had run Russia, often with little thought to the needs of the rest of the people. Now the Communists had taken over and gotten rid of the czar, and they were out to punish the wealthy.

Boris and Catherine decided to try to escape to a farm they owned in the neighboring country of Finland. Just before they got to the border, they stopped at a friend's house.

When their friend opened the door and saw them, he whispered, "You must hide quickly! The Communists are right here in this house," and he shut the door before anyone could see the young couple.

The only place to hide was a nearby pigpen. Luckily, it had a roof over it. For three days the Baron and Catherine hid there, and finally they were able to make a dash for the Finnish border.

As they approached their farm, they saw many of the old servants coming toward them. At last they had reached safety.

But this was not to be. The servants had become Communists, and they arrested their former masters.

As Catherine waited, a prisoner on her own property, she began to understand the life that had made her family rich had kept most of the people poor. No wonder the servants were ready to change their lives.

"I hadn't realized that the voice of the people was indeed the voice of God," Catherine says. "My family acted as kind as most of the other nobles. Sometimes we would give things to our servants. But that was not enough. I had heard them crying for freedom, and I scarcely listened."

By the time she and Boris were able to escape

from Finland, Catherine had begun to know that God's justice meant more than the few gestures made by her family. Although she disagreed violently with the Communists—especially when they told the people not to believe in God—she realized that much of the Revolution was not the fault of the common person.

Catherine and Boris sailed to Scotland. Boris was ill from years of hardship, and Catherine nursed him. They had left Russia with less than fifteen dollars and a few pieces of jewelry. All they had of value was life itself and each other.

Jobs were hard to find for everyone, but finally Boris heard of a job as a landscape architect. It was across the sea in Canada. They both wished they could go back to Russia, but that was impossible. They wondered whether they should go all the way to Canada.

Catherine had been praying for something good to happen, and now she said to Boris, "It is the answer to prayer. It is the voice of God. He wants us to go to Canada. So—we'll go!"

Soon after they arrived in Toronto, a baby was born to them. His name was George. Even if Boris was still not well enough to work, something beautiful had come into their lives in this child.

Now Catherine had to find a way to support the family, and she decided to go to New York, where she had heard that there were better chances to earn a living.

When they got to New York, the only job she could find was in a laundry where the people were poorly underpaid. Because she now understood what poverty really meant, she organized a strike for higher wages. Catherine lost both the strike and her job, but she noticed something that disturbed her even more than these losses. Here in New York, many of the people who helped the strikers, brought them food, and gave them support were Communists. She had left Russia rather than live in a Communist country, and now she found that it was the Communists who seemed more concerned with the poor than any other groups. It bothered her that the people from the churches weren't there helping too.

After losing the laundry job, Catherine got work with a lecture bureau. She traveled around the country on what was called the Chautauqua circuit, going from town to town talking about her life in Russia. Many people came to hear her, for she had always been a good speaker.

Soon she found herself in a top position with the lecture bureau, and she was wealthy again. After so many hard years, most people would have been relieved and happy, and for a time, Catherine was glad to be able to relax and not have to worry so much.

Before long, though, she began to have doubts about what her success really meant. Did God save me from death in Russia only to become rich in North America? she wondered as she prayed for guidance. Was it for this that God taught me to understand the terrible needs of the poor?

She asked for some answer. The only one she could hear seemed to say, in the words of Jesus, "Sell all you possess and give it to the poor and come, follow me."

After more than a year of prayer and planning, that is exactly what Catherine did. The year was 1931, the middle of the Great Depression; Boris had died of consumption. She and her son George went to live in the slums of Toronto. Now she would not simply think about the poor; she would be one of them.

When she went, she was only one person. "My only idea was to follow God's word. Soon others joined me. We lived together in a house we called Friendship House."

Before too long, other similar houses opened in different towns. Her example seem to draw people to share the life of helping the poor. Catherine tried to describe why this happened. "We became like a bonfire on top of a mountain. Many people see the light and come to find out what it is."

Others talk about the role Catherine herself played, both then and now. "She is a living flame, touched by the fire of God."

Praying for the poor is an important part of life at Friendship House. Catherine and her friends also help the poor in other ways. They perform what the Bible calls the works of mercy: feeding the hungry, clothing the naked, and taking care of the sick.

Catherine went to New York to start a Friendship House in Harlem, a section where many poor blacks lived. She tried to get other people involved. Like her friend Dorothy Day, she wanted people who read the church's teaching on social justice to really live it.

Many famous people came to visit Catherine. She was happy to see them, but she always reminded everyone never to judge even the most suspicious person at the door. "Even the most evil among us has some redeeming feature. Faith will seek it out."

In 1943, Catherine married Eddie Doherty, a newspaperman. In 1947, they left the large cities and went to Combermere, Ontario, a small town almost two hundred miles northeast of Toronto.

Once again, they were starting with nothing. But that was not new to Catherine. "On the first day, we made an act of faith. We planted apple trees. Somehow, we knew we had come home."

The first years was hard, and the couple often wondered why they stayed. Then they would think of the trees they had planted and of the God who could make trees—and dreams—grow wherever they were planted.

Soon other people joined them, and this Friendship House was called Madonna House, after Mary. No matter what the reason for a particular house, or where it was located, one thing was always the same. The front door was always painted blue, in honor of Mary, the Mother of God. There is an old saying that anyone who passes through such a door will be blessed.

"Combermere is the most beautiful place on earth," Catherine would tell Eddie. "It's like being in Heaven for a time."

By the 1970s, there were almost twenty Friendship Houses scattered across the Western Hemisphere from the Yukon to the West Indies.

Madonna House now has its own *poustinia*, "the place of the hermit," much as Catherine remembered it from her childhood. The whole Friendship

House movement is based on a balance between prayer—often done in these simple huts—and caring for other people. Today the focus is on migrant workers, native population, and whatever other needs come along. The guiding force, as always, is a strong belief in the God whom Catherine first met in Russia. This God tells us that we need to do two things together. One or the other alone is never enough. We must pray always, and we must live that prayer by helping all those who need help.

Catherine Doherty has spent her life doing that. Just how it is to be managed is not always clear. "At times I am confused," she laughs. "But I leave it all to God."

Mother
Teresa

"A Call within a Call"

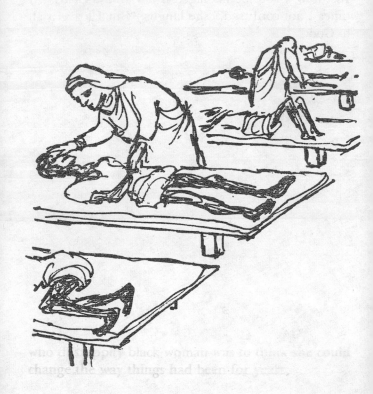

8

She does not look much like the saint that many claim her to be. She is tiny, barely five feet tall, with wrinkled skin and a crooked nose. Her voice is often heard in laughter, but her friends say she knows how to be pushy when there's something she wants done.

"She won't listen to anyone who says something is impossible," says one of her friends. "That makes her hard to live with sometimes, but it may also be one of her greatest strengths."

Mother Teresa is the founder of the Missionaries of Charity, who work with the poorest of the poor in India and around the world.

She was born Agnes Gouxha Bejaxhvi, of an Albanian family, in the town of Skopje in 1910. At that time, Skopje was part of Turkey. Now the boundaries have changed, putting it in the country of Yugoslavia. Her father was a grocer, and after his death, her mother continued to keep the business going.

"I learned how to work hard as a child," says Mother Teresa. "And I think that the idea of helping others came from our people, our own family. My mother was devoted to Jesus, and she taught us to pray."

Turkey was a largely non-Catholic country, and Agnes and her sister and brother grew up with people of many faiths or of no faith at all. When Agnes joined a girls' group at the local church, she began to hear reports of the work that missionaries were doing in India, and by the time she was twelve, she had already decided to spend her life helping the poor. Within a few years, after learning more about India, Agnes felt that God was calling her to go there to serve.

Home was a happy place for the Bejaxhvi family. Leaving it was the hardest thing Agnes had ever done, but her desire to become a nun in India was strong. When she turned eighteen, she joined the Sisters of Loretto, who operated schools in India, but first she went to Dublin, Ireland, to study at the Loretto convent there. In 1928, Agnes Gouxha Bejaxhvi left Ireland and headed, at last, for the land she had dreamed of so long—India. She took with her the name she had chosen to be called as a new sister. It was Teresa.

The young Sister Teresa landed in Calcutta, a city that was to play a vital role in her life, but at the time she didn't even have a chance to look around. She had to quickly board a train that took her to the Loretto convent at Darjeeling, India, at the base of the beautiful Himalayan Mountains.

As a new teaching nun, Teresa was not aware of the hard life led by millions of people in India. She taught in a clean convent school, and her pupils were not the poor she had planned to serve, but rather the children of the British who ruled the country or of the Indian upper class. Teresa accepted the position she found herself in without complaint. After all, she reasoned, it was not for her to investigate social conditions. To Sister Teresa, inside the safety of the convent gates, life seemed calm and orderly.

Darjeeling was one of the most comfortable cities in India. It has a pleasant climate. The rich vacationed there, for it was cooler in the summer than in the southern cities.

The situation was different in Calcutta. It had long been a city known for contrasting ways of life. There were extremely wealthy people in Calcutta, and there were many more who were desperately poor.

For the poor, life was always a struggle, but it was made worse when the monsoon season struck. From June until September, the rains drenched people as they huddled against buildings or in doorways for shelter.

The time was growing closer when Sister Teresa's childhood desire to serve the poor would become a reality, and in 1931 she was sent to teach at Saint Mary's Convent School in Calcutta. Teresa taught geography and helped run the school. Life here, it seemed, would be a repeat of the even pace she had known in Darjeeling.

One day Teresa wandered outside the convent grounds. She had been noticing a rotten odor in the air and she decided to investigate. It was coming from the Moti Jheel, the worst *bustis*, or slum, in Calcutta.

The young teacher was appalled. Everywhere she looked she saw filth and garbage. In the midst of this were shacks where the luckier of the poor lived, but many of the people had no shelter at all.

Something upset Teresa more than the odor and the dust. For the first time, the girl from Skopje was seeing the poor face-to-face. She watched people, young and old, digging in garbage to find food, or sitting there waiting, just waiting, to die of starvation.

Deeply moved, Teresa returned to the Moti Jheel and to the other slums of Calcutta as often as possible. She knew that something must be done to help these people. She prayed for them, as she had prayed all her life, but she knew that prayer was not enough. "Prayer without action is no prayer at all," Teresa told her friends at the convent, and she asked for and received permission to try to find a way to help.

Taking some of the students from her school, Teresa set out to visit Calcutta's hospitals and slums. It was demanding and exhausting work, but no matter what sickening things they saw during the day, the group knew they would be returning to their clean beds in the convent at night.

Teresa began to wonder whether she couldn't do more. Even though the Loretto nuns took the traditional vows of poverty, chastity, and obedience, their lives were not really difficult. They always had enough to eat and a clean place to sleep.

Teresa turned to prayer for a sign of what she should do. By now it was 1946. World War II had come and gone, and India was moving away from British rule and would soon become an independent nation.

Teresa prepared to make her annual visit, or retreat, to the Loretto convent in Darjeeling. As usual, she boarded the train for the overnight trip, but this year there was no chance of sleep for her. As the land sped by in the dark, Teresa thought about the lives of the poor people she had seen. By the time the journey to Darjeeling was over, a new journey had begun which would change the lives of thousands of people—starting with Sister Teresa herself.

Sometime during the night's ride, Teresa heard the answer to all her prayers about what she could do to help the poor. God seemed to have a plan for her.

"I decided I must leave the convent and be with the poor all the time. Somehow, I knew that was God's will and I had to follow him. It was to be his work."

In 1928, when she was eighteen years old, Agnes Gouxha Bejaxhvi had become Sister Teresa, a sister of Loretto. Now another eighteen years had passed, and she heard a voice leading her into a new form of service.

"My vocation to become a nun was from God. Now I heard a call within a call," Teresa told the superiors in her order when she returned to Calcutta from Darjeeling. She was ready to start her new life. Receiving permission to go out among the poor whom she had come to love, she left the secure world of the convent. She had no money, no training, not even a place to sleep at night. All Teresa had was her faith in God and a great desire to live that faith among the poor.

After a brief period of medical training, Teresa

was ready to begin her work. The week before Christmas in 1948, she started a school in the Moti Jheel. It was in the open air, for there was no building. The teacher drew in the dirt with a stick, for there were no books. The teacher was Teresa.

People began to hear about her work and offered to help with supplies and money, and soon she had the use of a building. Best of all, people came to work with her themselves. Many had known her when she had been their teacher at Saint Mary's School.

Before two years had gone by, there were enough women who had joined her to start their own order. It was named the Missionaries of Charity. As a sign of her commitment to be one with the poor, Teresa had begun wearing the dress of the poor Bengali women of India. To this day, the clothing of her Missionaries of Charity remains the same—a *sari,* or robe, of coarse white cotton, with a blue border. On her left shoulder, Teresa pinned a crucifix.

The order remained very poor. Even though it was often necessary to beg in order to raise money, Mother Teresa, as she was now called, did not lose hope.

"No matter how much we needed money, we never gave up. God always helped, and the people gave."

The life to which God had called Teresa and her new sisters was not an easy one. Their day still starts at 4:30 in the morning. The early hours are spent in prayer and at mass. After a simple breakfast, the missionaries begin another day of service.

To become a member of their order, a person

must meet four requirements: she must be healthy, have common sense, be able to learn, and have a good sense of humor. All four items are necessary to continue living among such poverty.

Members of most religious orders make three vows, or promises, when they choose their way of life. These are the vows of poverty and chastity and obedience. The Missionaries of Charity have the same rules; however, their vow of poverty is unusually strict.

"To be able to love the poor and know the poor, we must be poor ourselves," Teresa tells those who come to join. "We also have a fourth vow in which we promise to give wholehearted service to the poorest of the poor. We take no money, make no salary for serving people."

Once the school was going strong, Teresa began to turn her attention to some of the other problems in the troubled country.

She organized leper colonies to help the victims of this ancient disease find a place where they would be welcome. Another big problem was that of unwanted babies. More and more children were being born whose mothers were unable to take the responsibility of raising them. Some of these abandoned babies were brought to Mother Teresa by the midwives who had helped at their birth. Others were found in garbage cans, where they were thrown away as worthless pieces of nothing.

As more and more of the babies came to live with the sisters of the Missionaries of Charity, orphanages were begun. Many of the children were eventually adopted by people in India and around the world, although others still remain trapped in the poverty of their origins.

One of the main works of the Missionaries of Charity is their care for the dying. This act of mercy had its beginnings one day in 1954 when Mother Teresa was walking in front of a hospital. Suddenly, she saw a woman who was almost dead on the street. Rats and ants were already chewing on her body.

Mother Teresa picked the woman up and went into the hospital to get some help for her. The hospital staff didn't want to admit her because she had no money and couldn't pay the bill. They told Teresa that the woman would soon be dead, and they didn't want to be bothered.

Refusing to leave until the staff agreed to admit the woman, Teresa was saddened, for she knew people were dying every day on the streets of Calcutta alone and in misery.

She went to the city government, and asked for a building, and the Missionaries of Charity began their house for the dying. It is called *Nirmal Hriday*, the "Immaculate Heart."

The small building they were given had been a Hindu temple, and before the day was over, the sisters had moved in, bringing with them the dying poor they had gathered from the streets.

"We help the poor die with God," Mother Teresa told the Indians who asked her why she had opened the house. "We live that they may die with dignity."

Some of the people who come to the house do get well and leave. Before they go, the sisters give them some job training so they can have a chance to improve their lives.

In the fall of 1979, Calcutta's largest newspaper proclaimed: "The Mother of Bengal is now the Mother of the World." Mother Teresa has been named the winner of the Nobel Peace Prize for 1979.

Her answer to the questions of news reporters from all around the world: "I do nothing; He does it all." Standing firm in her belief in a loving God who calls her to serve his poor, she was able to say: "The prize is not for me . . . it is for the poor and I am receiving it in their behalf, is that not so?"

In accepting the award she asked that the abundant and rich banquet normally given for the Nobel Peace Prize winner be canceled. She requested that the money that would have been spent for the feast be used to feed the poor. She further stated that the $190,000.00 in prize money would be spent for the building of more schools and hospitals, and even on land and houses for the poor children who had grown to adulthood.

For Mother Teresa, this award was truly a peace prize. The love of the poor is an act of peace, for, as she said, "poverty and hunger and distress also constitute a threat to peace."

In her acceptance speech she encouraged us to love one another as God loves each of us. Through this award, the world was once more made aware of the power of love. Mother Teresa did not condemn the rich and affluent. She offered them her love and encouraged them to reach out to others in need.

Even though the work is endless and tiring, Mother Teresa never thinks of turning away and pretending she doesn't see what's going on.

Her critics say that it might be better if these people were left to die. They say that India has too many people for her resources now, so why work to save a life that is not of much value anyway?

Mother Teresa's answer is simple. "That way is not for us; our way is to preserve life, the life of Christ in others."

Her answer is the key to why she has kept at this work for so long. Mother Teresa does not act out some kind of grim guilt. She finds joy in her life, saying, "The poor do not need pity, but love and compassion. Give your hands to serve them, and your hearts to love them. You will be richly rewarded, for I believe we need the poor as much as they need us."

Dolores Huerta

"Look Up to God"

9

"Just one more dance!" Dolores's dark hair gleamed in the light as she turned to her friends.

"We have a lot of work to do tomorrow," Maria argued. "Let's go, we need some sleep."

But as the music started again, Maria shrugged and agreed to stay five more minutes.

Her friends learn quickly not to try to change Dolores Huerta's mind. Her nickname is La Pasionaria, which is Spanish for "the passionate one." It fits her well. Whether she is dancing or fighting for the cause of the farm worker in America, rarely does she do anything in a passive manner.

Her story begins in 1930, in Dawson, New Mexico, where she was born Dolores Fernandez. Her black hair and dark eyes reflect her ancestry, which is Indian, Mexican, and Spanish.

Dolores's father work in the mines of the Southwest until he was blacklisted for engaging in union activity. The blacklist was a list of names of "troublemakers"—people who tried to organize unions—to see if a worker's name was on it before they hired him or her. They would not hire anyone whose name was on it. Because of this, Mr. Fernandez left mining and became a migrant worker.

Later on, Dolores's parents were divorced, and she and her mother moved to Stockton, California. Her mother ran a restaurant and hotel where many farm workers and their families often stayed without charge because they were too poor to pay the rent.

When Dolores was growing up, she wanted to be a dancer. Instead in 1948 when she was eighteen years old, she married and had children. When she was a little older, she decided to go to college, and she got her teaching certificate, but her plans changed once again, and she began working with Mexican-Americans. As a result of that work, her whole life took on a new direction.

Many Mexican-Americans in California were farm workers, or migrants. To *migrate* means to move from one place to another, and that is what they did as they followed the crops from one field to the next. Wherever there were fields to be harvested, that is where they traveled.

Although migrants were of all races, many of them were Chicanos, or Mexican-Americans. It was their job to pick the tomatoes, grapes, lettuce, and other foods that grew in the rich California soil.

The farm workers, called *campesinos*, and the growers needed each other. In order to live, the workers needed whatever wages they could earn, and the growers needed people to pick the crops at exactly the proper time. Some growers cared about the workers, and they provided good houses for the campesinos and plenty of hot water and soap for showers at the end of a hot, dirty day.

Other growers cared more about the crops than about the workers. Without proper housing, the workers couldn't stay healthy. The pesticides that were used to kill the insects on the plants were often harmful to the workers, and their lungs and skin would burn. Some supervisors, who were hired by the growers, even charged a fee for a drink of water to cool off after working in the hot sun.

The workers felt that they had little choice but to do whatever the growers told them to do. The pay was low, but if a worker objected, she or he was fired. There were always plenty of *braceros* waiting for a chance to work. The braceros were brought in from Mexico, and they were even poorer than the American migrants. Because their families waited desperately in Mexico for them to send money, the braceros would do whatever the growers wanted without any questions.

The children of the worker families suffered the most. Although child labor laws had been enacted in most other industries, it was still legal for children to work all day long beside their parents in the fields. Their paychecks, as small as they were, were needed so the family could make enough money to live. Usually, the children went to school only in the winter, when no crops were waiting to be harvested. Because these children were so poorly educated, the future seemed to hold little hope for them getting out of the fields. It had gone on like this for generations.

Dolores saw this happening to the families who stayed at her mother's hotel, and she was disturbed by what she saw. She decided to find out what she could do about it, and in 1955, she began working with a group called the Community Service Organization (CSO) which was trying to help Mexican-Americans. The goal of the CSO was to teach people how to help themselves.

They worked for the hiring of a greater number of Chicano police, for better community centers, and for more effective city services. Because many of the Chicanos spoke little or no English, Dolores and the others from CSO worked toward establishing requirements for hospitals and other public agencies to employ people who could speak Spanish. If a mother brought a sick child to a hospital, there was a need for someone who would be able to help her, no matter what language she spoke.

What the CSO was trying to do went far beyond getting more material things for people. Dolores knew that, more importantly, the migrant families needed to have control over what happened to them. The people didn't believe that they could take control over their own lives. They were emotionally beaten, and they needed to gain confidence.

"You need to get some power," she would tell them. "Now, you might think *power* is a bad word. No! Power is good when it lets people choose what they want to do with their lives."

Slowly, the workers began to see that her ideas made sense.

A man by the name of Cesar Chavez began to work for the CSO. He and Dolores were both Mexican-American Catholics who wanted to help their people.

Cesar's parents had been migrants, and he and his brothers had worked in the fields. If anyone knew how much help the farm workers needed, it was Cesar. He and Dolores began to talk about this, and they agreed that the time had come to form a union for campesinos. The lives of these people must be made better.

In 1962, they decided to begin their work. The Community Service Organization had been a good training ground for both of them, but now it was time to move on.

They were well aware that the work would be hard. Cesar told Dolores, "You'll have to quit your job. You can't work for a living and fight this battle at the same time. It's one or the other. You choose."

Dolores cared about the workers, and she made the decision to quit her job. There was no salary; at times there wasn't even money to buy food. The people helped each other out, and the groundwork for a union went on.

Dolores loved her family very much, but she also loved her work. She would have to figure something out. Many times, her children would stay with friends or union members while their mother was busy.

Dolores wishes she had more time to spend with them. "I love my kids," she says. "In my culture, raising kids is the most important thing you can do. I'm working for their future. It's hard to balance everything, but we try."

Because she doesn't act like the traditional housewife, Dolores has been severely criticized. In the Mexican culture, women, even if they work in the fields along with their husbands, are expected to stay in the background.

Dolores couldn't do this, but despite her hectic

schedule, she always tries to find time with her family. "I want my children to be able to settle down in one place. The children in the field look down at the soil all day. They should also learn to look up to God. Maybe our union will give them a chance to do that."

Because they believed in their ideal so much, Dolores and Cesar took the step. They had left the CSO. Now they formed the National Farm Workers Association (NFWA), called *La Causa* among the workers. This organization would become more than a job for Dolores and the others. It was their cause, their future for which they were fighting.

Although higher wages were important, Cesar and Dolores knew that the farm workers needed more than money. They needed to start looking at their lives differently. "We must change people's lives," the union leaders would tell each other. "Once they see that they can make things happen, then we will have a strong union."

In the fall of 1965, the members of the NFWA voted to strike in support of a group led by Larry Itliong, a friend from CSO days. This strike was of Filipino workers against grape growers who paid different workers different wages for the same work. The Filipino workers made less than the braceros. Both made less than the Anglos, or whites.

"Equal pay for equal work! *Huelga!* Strike! *Viva la Causa!*" The workers shouted their support as the first major strike among farm workers was about to begin.

For Dolores, this was an exciting and rewarding moment. Although the struggle was long and hard,

98

the workers were beginning to show their power.

When people from across the country began to hear about the strike, some of the other unions of many churches and individuals volunteered their help. Without the assistance of so many, the strike could not have lasted too long.

In the end, twelve companies signed an agreement with the strikers. The NFWA joined with Larry Itliong's group to form the United Farm Workers Union (UFW). Together, they were stronger than ever. Chavez was elected president. Dolores was the first vice-president.

Chavez has often been criticized for not giving any woman except Dolores top positions in the union. However, almost fifty percent of the organizers are women, and they are in charge of many of the union programs. This is especially impressive in the Mexican culture, where women traditionally have stayed at home.

"Women are very important to La Causa," says Dolores. "Unless the woman supports the union, the men in the family usually don't either."

Belonging to the union is definitely a family affair. Dolores's children have grown up taking part in whatever was happening. When her son Emilio was nine years old he smuggled leaflets in to some women farm workers after the union had been forbidden to come onto a grower's property. He had to run a quarter mile to get out because the grower's manager was chasing him in a car. But Emilio was proud. The UFW was fighting for his future, too, and he was part of the fight.

For Chavez, Huerta, and the migrant workers,

winning meant more than higher wages and better housing. It was a matter of justice. Before a strike began, Dolores would hold up a crucifix. Everyone touched it, pledging themselves to support the strike. They believed that what they were doing was holy in the sight of God.

Sometimes her involvement with the union has placed Dolores in danger. One day the car she was riding in broke down out in the country. They stopped at a house to ask for help, and it turned out to be the house of a grower. He opened the door, all right, but not to offer help. He had a shotgun in his hands, and as he came outside he fired it into the air. Dolores quickly left.

As the United Farm Workers grew, Dolores traveled more frequently beyond California. In other states, she found that the workers weren't as hopeful. They hadn't seen the success that was possible.

And they didn't know what a fighter they had in Dolores. Sometimes, it was hard to convince the workers that their lives were worth the fight. They had been treated as less than human for such a long time that they were starting to believe it no longer mattered what happened to them.

Dolores knew that this attitude was a deadlier enemy than all the growers' tricks ever could be. She believed that God intended workers to have a good life, too, and she knew she must make the workers understand and accept that.

She would tell the campesinos, "We can win."

They would shake their heads sadly and say, *"No se puede."* That is Spanish for "it's not possible."

But Dolores wouldn't let them give up so easily. She began to tell them over and over again, "*Sí, se puede*—yes, we can!"

Slowly, more and more farm workers have begun to believe in the union and in themselves. Conditions are improving, although the battle is not nearly over.

"Justice is won over and over again," Dolores says. "No one is going to win their battle for them. Farm workers' conditions can be changed by only one group—themselves."

Dolores Curran

"I'm Here for a Purpose"

10.

It was a sunny Wisconsin summer day, and Dolores Fox was wandering along the country road that ran past her family's farm. She was on her way to visit her friend who lived on the farm next door. Ernie was an old man, and he lived with his son, but Dolores liked to talk to him because he had grown up with her grandma who was dead now. Ernie often told her how much she looked like Minnie, her grandma, and sometimes he would tell her stories about the games they used to play.

As Dolores skipped into the room where Ernie sat in his favorite chair, she could see that he was sleeping, so she turned around to leave.

Ernie woke with a start. "Why, Minnie!" he called out, his face looking young and happy again.

Dolores knew what had happened. For a minute, coming out of his sleep, Ernie had thought that she was her grandma. For just an instant there, he had been young again with someone who had shared his life.

She stood still, not quite knowing what to say.

"Oh, no. It's Dolores. Now I see." Ernie sounded a little sad, and Dolores watched as the light dimmed in his eyes and he seemed to shrivel into an old man again.

Dolores was fascinated and excited by the way Ernie had changed from age to youth and back again. Later, when she tried to explain to her family what she had seen, they listened politely, but they didn't really understand how important this moment had been to her.

Things like that happened often to Dolores. Now that she is older and has become a writer, she realizes that early on she had begun to develop the habit of looking at life in a special way, of seeing things a little differently.

"It seems like I've spent my lifetime watching what happens around me and then thinking about how I feel about it. Other writers have told me that they do the same thing, but when I was young, all I knew was that I seemed to notice things that no one else thought important."

Today, Dolores is a successful writer of books, as well as a syndicated newspaper columnist, and she travels around the country speaking to groups about the importance of family life.

It's a long way from her beginnings on a dairy farm in Wisconsin, but Dolores knows that the events of her childhood are part of the reason for what she has become today.

She was born on February 11, 1932, in Edgerton, Wisconsin, where her family lived on the land that her ancestors had farmed for generations. There were seven children in the family, so there was always someone to play with. Her parents, William and Lillian Fox, maintained a strong Catholic faith.

"Belief was especially strong right at home," says Dolores. "There weren't any Catholic schools for us to attend, but that was a good thing because we learned about the importance of our religion from our parents. We prayed together and talked about God very naturally while we were growing up."

Like other Irish-Catholic families in America, the Fox family enjoyed many traditions. They planted their potatoes on Good Friday and had oyster stew on Christmas Eve.

In addition to these customs, the Foxes had special traditions all their own. On Easter Sunday afternoon Dolores's father would take his seven children and walk from field to field, blessing the earth with holy water. As he explained what would be planted in each field, the kids reached down and gathered up handfuls of soil, and as it ran through their fingers, they felt close to their land and to the God who helped the crops grow.

Dolores was a middle child. Sometimes she seemed to get lost in the crowd. "I was the one nobody could quite remember," she says, laughing. "I think that might be why I grew up to have such a strong drive to do something—then people would remember!"

As she grew older, Dolores decided that she wanted to leave the farm. One of the main things she had in mind was to become a writer. She had so many ideas for stories. People would tell her she was too sensitive, but she couldn't help noticing what went on around her. Someday, she dreamed, she would be able perhaps to share her feelings and observations with others!

Dolores always carried a pencil and paper. She was a good student, and when she graduated from high school in 1949, she wanted more education.

Her family earned a decent living from the farm and they were not poor, but there was never much money to spare. In order to send their children to college, the Foxes made a deal with each one as the time came to leave home.

"We will give you the money you need," her father would say, "if you promise to pay it back in two years after graduation, so the next one can go to school, too."

Dolores was used to hard work, and she didn't mind this arrangement. At first, she studied designing and sewing. Then she discovered that it was her English and literature courses that excited her more than any others, so she decided to become an English teacher.

After she graduated from the University of Wisconsin, she taught for two years and paid her parents back, as she had agreed. At last, at the age of twenty-four, she was ready to start life on her own. She and her sister Dottie had applied for and accepted teaching jobs in California, and they decided to spend the summer in Colorado. It was a good time for the sisters because they were doing what they wanted and soon they would be teaching subjects they loved. One night while they were in Colorado, the two girls went to a rodeo with their dates. It was wonderful just to relax and have fun after the hard years of studying and working.

On the way home from the rodeo, their car was in a terrible accident. Of the four people in the car, Dolores was the only one who was seriously injured. In just a few seconds, her whole life had changed. Now she was in a Colorado hospital with a broken neck and a badly injured arm. All her plans for the future were turned around.

There are moments in everyone's life when they question their faith. For Dolores, this was such a time. She had always been such an independent person, and now she had to ask for help in everything she did. Although it was a hard time for her, she found that there were many good people who were willing to help.

Even though Dolores would have to wear a cast on her arm for an entire year, the school system of Englewood, Colorado, decided to hire her as a junior high school teacher.

Dolores had always been an active person, and here she was in Colorado, one of the main ski areas in the country, and she couldn't participate. She couldn't even take a bath without help.

Soon she became so bored with her life that she decided to find something to do, and she signed up at the local public school to attend an adult education class in writing. She recalled her childhood dream of becoming a writer. Maybe now she would have the chance.

The first assignment was to write an article and try to get it published. Using one hand, Dolores pecked away at her typewriter and sent her article off to the local newspaper. To her delight, the article was accepted! She was the first person of all in her class to sell something, and soon she was selling other stories.

"It was a great gift from God that I sold something so quickly," Dolores believes. A whole new area opened up, her long recovery back to becoming her usual healthy self passed more quickly as she began to write.

Soon after her writing began to get published, Dolores met Jim Curran. Dolores was twenty-six years old and Jim was twenty-eight when they were married in 1958. They had both been teaching and were ready to start a family, but it was three and a half years before Teresa was born. Later, they had two sons, Patrick and Dan.

"I'm a strong believer in God's plan," Dolores recalls. "If our children had been born early in our marriage, as we wanted, they would have been grown up by the time all the exciting changes were going on in the Catholic Church, and we would have missed out."

When Teresa was born, Dolores gave up her teaching and stayed home, as did most mothers in those days. She began writing seriously.

"I tried to be content with being a housewife and mother. I really tried, and soon I felt guilty because I wanted something more." Thinking back over the changes society has gone through in the years since then, she says, "Today, I don't think I would have had to feel so alone."

Jim had known Dolores as a teacher and writer before they were married, so he always knew that she could do whatever she wanted. He pitched in and helped with the children.

As the 1960s unfolded, Dolores and Jim got involved in the local human relations organization. They worked together for fair housing, interracial justice, and peace in Vietnam. The women's movement began to affect their lives more and more.

During this time, Dolores wrote about these issues for newspapers and magazines, and before long, she was writing a weekly column. Her current column, "Talks with Parents," appears weekly in fifty-two Catholic papers.

As the Currans became familiar with the kinds of problems that the world was facing, they both realized that the individual family would have to play a dominant role in any changes for the better that could take place in our lives. Since 1974, Dolores has devoted most of her time and energy to working for and writing about the importance of the family and the necessity for adults taking responsibility for their own lives.

In 1971, Dolores Curran was the only American mother to attend the First Catechetical Congress in Rome, a meeting of Catholics from all over the world who were interested in religious education. It was exciting for her to see all of these people working together on the same ideas.

Over the years, Dolores has written several books that stress the importance of the individual, especially the idea of parents as people. Although she travels and lectures, she considers writing her true vocation.

To her, writing is a real ministry—a way of serving other people.

"You never know what influence you have on people as a writer, though," she admits. "If I did something more in line with the work of Mother Teresa or Dorothy Day, I might be able to see more tangible results. Writing is a less tangible ministry."

Dolores has had considerable influence on her

women readers. "It's so important that we get people, especially in church leadership, to see that God created women, too. Women have more to offer than simply being there to clean the altar or run bazaars.

"We look at our daughters and know their world will have changed even more than ours has. Then we look at our sons and wonder what kind of girls they will meet. We aren't doing our children any favors by not preparing them for the future."

For Dolores, part of this preparation for the future is in her public work of writing and speaking. But she also needs time to herself.

"Prayer is very important to me," she explains. "I keep it informal, but that doesn't mean it's not important. Instead of praying at a certain time each day, I meditate in the car, or I pray while working at home."

Dolores has been a good model for many women today. She has a full life with her husband and children, and she continues to do the work that suits her talents. "I'm a great believer in the Holy Spirit. I think probably the reason all of this has happened to me is that the people in the pew at church needed someone who could speak their language. I look at the official documents and then try to put them into the language of the home."

When she speaks out, she doesn't worry that she is not as formally educated as someone who spent years in a seminary. "I don't have any great theological background. I just take the insights and skill that God has given me and try to put them all together. I try to be a translator between official religion and home religion. I don't really see myself as having any other great value."

To the people in the pew, the ordinary men and women who make up the church, there is value enough in her writings.

Week after week, she gives them the kind of information they need in order to make decisions about how best to live their lives. When she tells them that she is hopeful for the future, it gives them hope of their own.

"My faith tells me that I'm here for a purpose and that God isn't going to abandon us. I was taught in my childhood that God works through us. We'd better get busy and do our part to help out his plan."

For the young women who are trying to decide how to have a husband and a family and still use their talents, Dolores seems part of God's plan, too.

Mairead Corrigan

"Something Happened in Belfast Today"

11.

On a hot August day in 1976, ten thousand Catholic and Protestant women marched down the streets of Belfast, the capital city of Northern Ireland, demanding an end to the fighting and killing that was going on in their country. The march itself was unusual enough, but what was really surprising was that Catholics and Protestants were working together on anything at all. In Northern Ireland, they generally came together only to fight each other.

Throughout the whole country, television newscasters spread the word of what had happened. It was the start of the Peace People movement.

It might be hard for us in America to understand why this march by people of two different religions was so special. We are used to living and playing and working with people who go to many different churches, or to no church at all.

But in Northern Ireland, the first thing you learn about people is whether they are Catholic or Protestant. Until recently, the two groups have stayed separate. Except during periods of violence, many people have grown up in Northern Ireland and never known anyone of a different religion.

In 1976, a woman named Mairead Corrigan

joined many others to try to change this violent way of living. She is part of the Peace People movement of Northern Ireland. For the first time in Irish history, Catholics and Protestants are working together to bring peace to their country.

To understand why this cooperation was so badly needed, it is necessary to know a little bit about this beautiful and sad land.

For such a small island, Ireland has had an unhappy and complicated past. The Irish and the English have battled each other for centuries. So have the Catholics and the Protestants. In 1922, the island was officially divided into two countries.

The northern six counties (called Ulster, or Northern Ireland) stayed part of the United Kingdom. The southern section became the Republic of Ireland, which is also called Eire and is almost all Catholic.

Although the North is made up mostly of Protestants, one-third of the people there are Catholic. Like many minorities, these Catholics have ended up with the lowest-paying jobs and the worst housing, although many of their Protestant countrypeople are little better off.

Even after the two countries came into existence, the fighting continued in the North. Groups of semimilitary organizations remained, each determined to achieve a position of power. The Catholic group was called the Irish Republican Army, or the IRA, the modern version of which is called the Provisionals, or Provos. The Protestant group was called the Ulster Defense League (UDL). Not all the citizens of Northern Ireland supported one of these groups, but people didn't stand against them either, and so the fighting continued.

The situation between the Catholics and the Protestants in Ulster is something like the relationship between the black and the white people in the United States before the civil rights movement began to ease matters. People hated and feared those on the other side, even if they had never had any personal contact with each other.

There were many reasons for people in Ulster to be so unhappy. Unemployment was high, especially among the Catholic minority, and they did not have much chance to say what kind of life they wanted to lead.

In 1969, the "troubles"—as the Irish call the fighting—were so bad that British troops moved into Northern Ireland to try to maintain order.

Another problem was the fierce loyalty to family and neighborhood that has always been a part of Irish culture. Irish people are traditionally close to their own small circle, but they tend to shut others out.

Even in recent times, Catholic and Protestant children grow up without ever knowing anyone who isn't of the same religion.

It is important to care about family and neighborhood, but when people forget to care about others, violence has a better chance of erupting. This is what happened in Ulster.

Mairead Corrigan was born into this kind of atmosphere in 1944. She was second in a family of seven children. Her father was a window washer and her mother was a housewife.

Mairead had a happy childhood. Unlike many people in Northern Ireland, her family had not suffered directly because of the troubles. Her older brother had emigrated to New Zealand, and they all missed him, but no one in the family had ever been killed or injured. Along with the other children in her area of Belfast, Mairead attended Catholic schools; the state-run schools taught the Protestant religion.

Both schools taught Irish history, but from different points of view. Each side said that they were completely right and the others completely wrong.

When Mairead was fourteen, her family could not afford for her to go on to high school. Instead, she attended business school for one year and she became a bookkeeper.

The Legion of Mary was an organization that she and many of her friends joined. They met to study their beliefs, and they learned to help others and to show the love of Christ by doing good works.

There was much that needed to be done in Belfast. The government-built housing projects where most Catholics lived weren't very comfortable or pleasant places. There were no stores or movies or parks, no places for people to meet and enjoy themselves.

Children quickly grew bored and prone to mischief. A favorite way to pass the time was to throw stones at the British soldiers who patrolled the area. The presence of these soldiers was enough to create hostility among the Irish, and the prankishness of the children throwing rocks was obviously an activity that led to fighting and violence. Community centers

116

were needed so that children could learn something besides fighting.

Mairead and her friends in the Legion of Mary got funds together and set up a nursery school and a place for handicapped children to play and learn. She was beginning to see that something more than wishful thinking was needed if there was going to be any improvement in her country.

Besides her Legion work, Mairead led an ordinary life. She worked, spent time with her family, and went out with her friends or on dates.

At home, the older people would talk about the old times and the fighting, but Mairead didn't pay much attention to their stories. She was young, and she had too many other exciting things to do than think about the past. Besides, most of the time, the fighting wasn't that bad in Ireland. Maybe the worst of times was over.

Then, in 1969, when Mairead was twenty-five years old, the troubles started again. Protestants and Catholics began to set fire to each other's houses. Mairead had heard of this happening in the past, but she was surprised to learn that it was happening now. Both sides were doing it.

This wasn't history. It was real. Her own aunt had to move out of her house because of the violence. The troubles grew more and more personal in terms of Mairead's life.

Once, when she was attending a Catholic funeral, British soldiers came into the church and threw tear gas on the altar. Her eyes burning from the gas, Mairead became very angry. She wondered what she could do. She didn't want to join the Provos, and she didn't know how to combat the situation without becoming violent herself.

Mairead prayed hard, but she found no quick answers, except that she couldn't imagine Jesus being violent.

People tried to tell her that she was doing all that was possible. After all, what could one woman do?

She didn't know. All she knew was that something had to be done.

Soon after this incident, the Legion of Mary began visiting the Long Kesh prison, where both Catholics and Protestants suspected of terrorist activities were held.

The women of the Legion tried to tell the prisoners that violence was not the answer. Mairead believed that most of these were good men, driven to fighting after seeing their families beaten or their parents' homes destroyed. A few, she knew, were in it only for the adventure.

The prisoners listened to what the women had to say, and then they said, "You are traitors to Ireland. It's easy for you to come here and say that you are right and we are wrong. You can leave here and not do any more about the troubles. You're cowards for not fighting along with us."

These men and their families were from the same land as Mairead. She had known some of them for years. It was hard for her to continue to speak out against the fighting. But she did.

Life continued much the same for Mairead, but the violence grew worse. Not only were more soldiers and members of the IRA and UDL being killed, but innocent people were dying too. A bomb

118

would blow up in a store, or a stray bullet would hit a child on the street.

Then, one day, something happened that changed Mairead Corrigan's life forever.

It was August 10, 1976. Anne Maguire, Mairead's sister, had gone out for a walk with her children. Jonna was eight years old and was pushing Andrew, the six-week-old baby, in his carriage. Two-year-old John held his mother's hand. It was a hot, dry day.

Suddenly a car jumped the curb and smashed into them, killing the three children and seriously injuring their mother.

The driver of the car, Danny Lennon, a member of the Provos, had been shot in the heart by British soldiers and was already dead when the car hit the children.

A woman named Betty Williams happened to be on the street, and she saw the children die. This "accident" was not all that unusual; it happened often in 1976.

What was unusual was that this time a few people decided to try to do something about the violence and the killing.

Mairead, grief stricken by the deaths in her own family, appeared on television and begged that the fighting stop.

Meanwhile, on her own, Betty Williams went from door to door asking people, "Do you want peace?"

Over six thousand people signed a petition, saying yes!

The Maguire family asked Betty Williams to attend the funeral of the three children. It was the first time that Mairead and Betty met each other. One of the news reporters at the funeral was Ciaran McKeown, and these three people joined together to start what became known as the Peace People movement.

Many people attended the services. The next day, ten thousand people (mostly women, but men joined them later on) marched through the streets of Belfast. There were no speeches, only prayers.

The remarkable thing was that Catholics and Protestants marched together. Both sides were sick of the killing. They weren't certain what they should do, they knew only that something had to be done.

For outsiders, the march was deeply moving to watch. For the Northern Irish, it was incredible. People from both sides were protesting the troubles in a peaceful march. The women were attacked and called traitors, but they kept marching.

This was the start of the Peace People movement. Mairead Corrigan would have plenty of chances now to see if she really believed the words she had told the men at Long Kesh.

Many people became involved with the Peace People, and the marches continued for the rest of the year. These were necessary to get people involved. Plans began for playgrounds, nurseries, and jobs. People were slowly beginning to see that not only *must* the violence stop, but that it *could* stop. Peace did have a chance.

In July 1977, Anne and Jack Maguire took their remaining son and moved to New Zealand to try to begin a new life.

Slowly, a new future is growing in Ulster. The

Peace People have won many awards, including the Nobel Peace Prize. They have been criticized by some, but they have made a start.

Mairead continues her work. "We just want ordinary men and women to join a peace group," she says. "I love my country very much, but I would give a hundred Irelands if only my sister could have her children with her again. People are important, not countries. Life is too precious to ever waste."

Northern Ireland's troubles aren't over yet. But neither is Mairead's faith in God. "I believe that God makes use of every one of us in a special way," Mairead says, and she has found her special way. The Peace People and Northern Ireland can be grateful that she has.

Epilogue

There are connections running between the stories of these great women. Mother Jones, for example, died in 1930—the same year that Dolores Huerta was born. And Dolores Huerta is working for the United Farm Workers, a group that has attracted the support of Dorothy Day. As we read today's newspapers and watch the television news, we are sure to learn more about these women and their causes.

For each of them, what happened in their lives was partially a result of the politics and economics of the times in which they lived. Sojourner Truth was able to influence people because she was a powerful woman, but also because the country was beginning to think about the slavery question. Corrie ten Boom's message of forgiveness probably would not have come about had she not lived in Holland during World War II.

As times change, so will the way in which women can make a difference. But individuals can always affect the world if they are willing to take the necessary risks to do so.

These women have characteristics in common. Many of them were not content to "stay in their

123

place," whatever that place happened to be for women in their situation. Jeannette Piccard refused to give up her dream, even if America of the early 1900s did not encourage "young ladies" to be ministers. Mother Teresa did not stay inside her comfortable convent walls, even though many decent nuns in India were doing just that.

None of these women waste time saying "if only" such and such had (or hadn't) happened. They accepted the situation as it was—and then set out to change it for the better. Elizabeth Seton could have spent the rest of her life believing that a young widow with five children simply couldn't be expected to help anyone else, and no one would have found fault with her decision. Mairead Corrigan could have vowed to work for peace, but only when the other side showed that they were ready too.

Instead, each one went ahead and did what she could. None waited to be handed the power, or the money, or the co-workers before she started to work for her dream. As many times as it was necessary, these women all changed their lives and started over. For Mother Jones, this meant beginning again after her family died, and again after the Chicago Fire, and again and again after the many times she was jailed.

Each of their lives was different. Some of the women seemed to see God everywhere, as did Corrie ten Boom and Mother Teresa. There were times when others couldn't see such goodness at all. Dorothy Day and Elizabeth Seton both felt abandoned at times in their lives. None of them knew at the beginning what shape their lives would take or where their work would lead.

For some, knowing other people gave them the strength to begin. Dorothy Day had Peter Maurin; Dolores Huerta met Cesar Chavez. Dolores Curran had the support of her husband Jim; Corrie ten Boom's family had raised her in love. Whether they worked alone, as did Sojourner Truth as she wandered the roads of America, or as part of a group, such as Elizabeth Seton's Sisters of Charity, they were never truly alone. They each knew that someone, somewhere, cared about what happened to them.

As I have learned about these women, I have been amazed that so few of them could accomplish so much. At the same time, it has shown me again that one person acting from a strong belief in God can begin to change her part of the world for the better.

I hope you have enjoyed this book and have learned something from these stories. I would love to hear from you to see what has impressed you most.

Please remember that you need only learn from others—you don't ever have to copy them. None of us has to be another Dorothy Day or Mother Teresa. That's their job. We don't have to be "just like" anyone in the whole history of the world, no matter how great that person is.

We just have to be ourselves, the very best that we can manage.

Elizabeth Seton	born 1774	died 1821
Sojourner Truth	1797	died 1883
Mother Jones	1830	died 1930
Corrie ten Boom	1892	
Jeannette Piccard	1895	
Dorothy Day	1897	died 1980
Catherine de Hueck Doherty	1900	
Mother Teresa	1910	
Dolores Huerta	1930	
Dolores Curran	1932	
Mairead Corrigan	1944	

5D